In the Kitchen with Bob

Coast to Coast

IN THE KITCHEN WITH BOB

Coast to

Coast

Bob Bowersox

Food photographs by Mark Thomas Studio

QVC PUBLISHING, INC.

QVC Publishing, Inc.
Jill Cohen, Vice President and Publisher
Ellen Bruzelius, General Manager
Karen Murgolo, Director of Acquisitions and Rights
Cassandra Reynolds, Publishing Assistant

Produced in association with Patrick Filley Associates, Inc.
Design by Joel Avirom and Jason Snyder
Photography by Mark Thomas Studio
Prop styling by Nancy Micklin
Food Styling by Ann Disrude
Text contributions by Judith Dern

Grateful acknowledgement is made to Martha Nesbit for the use of her peach
pound cake recipe on page 20.

Q Publishing and colophon are trademarks of QVC Publishing, Inc.

Published by QVC Publishing, Inc., 50 Main Street, Mt. Kisco, New York 10549

Manufactured in Hong Kong

ISBN: 1-928998-08-9

First Edition

10 9 8 7 6 5 4 3 2 1

Contents

Introduction

What defines American cuisine? With that simple question began a road trip. Throughout the year 2001 we took my QVC television show "In the Kitchen with Bob," coast to coast to nine different locations in search of the perfect recipe. It was a trip designed to explore the very best regional cuisine across the country, a chance to talk to local cooks and find out what really makes that region's food so special—and delicious!—and then highlight those regional secrets for home cooks like yourself. In short, to share with you my discoveries and try to define American cooking.

The first thing I learned on my cross-country exploration is that American cooking offers a remarkable diversity of ingredients, flavors and seasonings. These include the culinary traditions of our colonial forefathers from Great Britain and Western Europe, who often learned from Native Americans how to adapt Old World recipes to New World ingredients. It also includes foods and kitchen traditions brought by later arrivals from around the world. All of them learned to adapt and assimilate their cooking customs, tastes and techniques at first to what was grown, caught or hunted locally, and later to what was found on grocery store shelves, raised on the farm, grown in gardens, or imported.

What also became evident was just how blessed we are by America's fertile landscape and its abundance of foodstuffs. In the country's Midwestern agricultural heartland and California's Central Valley, along with many other areas of this country, there are amber fields of waving grain, acres of corn, orchards with every kind of fruit and vegetable imaginable, plus great ranches and farms raising cattle, pigs, sheep and poultry. Farmers large and small cultivate a tremendous variety of outstanding food products, so we have an amazing number of choices about what to eat and what ingredients to cook with—more so than anywhere else in the world.

Add to that the wonderful assortment of regional foods that are also available and our dining horizons expand further, at least when we visit someplace new and sample the local cuisine, or read about it in a cookbook or magazine and try out a new recipe at home. Regional foods are decidedly part of what defines American cooking, and the current enthusiasm for farmers markets, community supported agriculture, heirloom vegetables, and eating seasonally is yet another dimension of this interest in local cuisine.

The third thing that defines American cooking, at least for me, is attitude. In my travels coast to coast, I noted the enthusiasm and generosity of everyone for sharing their cooking with visitors. "Taste this, try that," my hosts would eagerly say, sharing their pleasure and urging me to learn from their knowledge or rediscovery about the history of their regional cuisine and what makes it so delicious. I found that we Americans know how to celebrate what's unique about a food, a tradition, or a region, and we do this with energy, open-handedness and a generous pride in sharing the best. I discovered some fabulous cooks out there and they are keeping alive the best traditions of our country's regional cuisine. For me, this celebration of native and heirloom ingredients and regional dishes—paired with a renewed appreciation for the historical events and immigration patterns shaping our country—plus the wonderful diversity of foods we have available, is as good a definition of American cuisine as any.

So I invite you to discover and taste what I learned about the variety, range of flavors and delicious styles of cooking that make up our country's regional cuisines. You'll find seafood recipes with the subtle Asian flavor of a spicy sake sauce paired with halibut from the Pacific Northwest and tender grilled shrimp prepared Napa Valley-style with cilantro and toasted pine nuts. You'll also find recipes for classic baked clams New England-style with bacon and white wine and a tasty lobster roll sandwich that will make you feel like you're lunching on the Maine coast. I've also included Savannah's favorite, Pecan-Crusted Catfish. Its crunchy nut coating makes it a real favorite of mine.

There are also main courses that may be familiar, such as chicken pot pie and strip steak, but prepared the traditional way they do in New England and Kansas City, each has a delicious new personality. Of course, I included crab cakes from Chesapeake Bay, seasoned with curry for a different twist. Then there are some classic regional main dishes like a shrimp jambalaya from New Orleans, as well as jerked chicken and pulled pork, both Jamaican-inspired favorites in the Florida Keys. I know you'll enjoy them all.

For side dishes, you'll find out how versatile beans are from one region to another. There's the New Orleans favorite, red beans and rice, along with refried beans made the authentic Southwestern way using bacon fat and pinto beans. From the Keys comes a savory Caribbean black bean salad made with the added punch of jalapeño peppers, cinnamon and allspice, and yes, I included a recipe for that Southern legend, fried green tomatoes.

Of course, there are desserts too! That's where regional cooks really try to outdo each other with cakes and pies that have America's history baked right in. You'll find an old-fashioned Shoofly Pie with 19th century origins in Pennsylvania Dutch kitchens. Or a praline sundae from New Orleans starring that city's favorite pecans in a seductive sauce that would make any flavor of ice cream swoon, but I recommend the richest vanilla you can buy. There's also a delicate fresh apricot soufflé from California's wine country and a buttery peach pound cake that's a Savannah hostess's prized recipe.

After all the miles traveled, all the towns and cities and homes visited, and all the recipes tasted in this coast to coast exploration, I think you'll be surprised at the range of styles and flavors, the outstanding ingredients, and the rich local food traditions in this collection of regional American recipes. Our country's history, its diverse ethnic influences over the centuries, and its ongoing community spirit are also ingredients in every one of these recipes. We truly enjoy some of the world's best home cooking and you can't give any cuisine much higher praise than that.

SAVANNAH

She-Crab Soup

Fried Green Tomatoes

Marilee's Fried Chicken

Candied Sweet Potatoes

Ham and Red-Eye Gravy

Skillet Corn Bread

Low Country Boil

Applesauce Cake

Pecan-Crusted Catfish

Martha Nesbit's Peach Pound Cake

I can't imagine a better place to have begun our year-long sampling of America's regional cuisines than in the South. There's something about the area that stretches from the Pennsylvania/Maryland line to Florida, from the Atlantic to the Mississippi that holds so much of what we like to think of as American. Then again, it might just be a matter of personal heritage.

You see, I was raised by a mother who considered herself a "southern belle." Everything she did in the kitchen or dining room was permeated with the sensibilities of the South. Beauty, grace, and hospitality were watchwords for mom. And twice a week at least, she graced our dinner table with her fried chicken—a simple recipe that I have still not found an equal to, no matter where in the South I've been.

More importantly, though, I'm convinced that the South is our country's best example of the concept of America as a "melting pot," particularly when you take that term in the culinary sense. For it is here that we find the most obvious blending of geography, climate, history, natural resources, and people into a cuisine. A cuisine that evolved naturally, easily absorbing and integrating many influences—even those from cultures a continent away.

One of the greatest "secrets" of Southern cuisine is that nothing is cooked that isn't at its peak of freshness. Because of the geography and climate, southerners don't have to worry about when things are right—they just have to be patient. They can pick the corn when it's bursting with sugars. They can pull a ruby-red tomato from the vine when it's just moments from delivering it's finest flavor. They can pinch off the sweetest, tiniest leaves of the okra and cook them immediately. This is why Southern cuisine explodes with flavor. The best southern recipes crop up by season—God hands southern cooks His perfection and they add their own humble touches combining ingredients in ways that few other American cooks do.

The earliest settlers were simple folk—farmers inland and fishermen along the coasts. They ate what they grew or caught. While pork was the honored meat, the early cuisine also embraced wild game like deer, turkey, quail, and duck. And shrimp, oysters, fish, and crab were also brought to the tables.

The rise of the cotton trade and the creation of huge plantations brought an influence that changed the cuisine forever. The slave trade, while abhorrent, brought ideas from other lands and added non-native ingredients like watermelon, okra, collard greens, and guinea hens.

Then came the Civil War. Staying alive in that time—for both the ruined plantation owners and the slave populations—brought all the cuisines together. They combined their ingredients and cooking into what could be called a "survival cuisine" that just kept "body and soul together" during the hard times. Nothing was wasted—every part of the pig, for instance, from fat, skin, and hocks, was used. And whatever the earth could grow, creative southern cooks found a way to use it. What we now call "soul food" was born.

And out of this great melding came southern cooking— a very passionate, very natural cuisine that harbors some of the richest flavors you'll come across. And if you love good food and great recipes, you'll love these.

She-Crab Soup

CRABS, PARTICULARLY BLUE CRABS, are a cult all up and down the Atlantic Coast, in the Chesapeake Bay where they reign, and even in the Gulf of Mexico. They are a delicacy enjoyed during the long fishing season from early spring through autumn. Although smaller than their West Coast cousin, the Dungeness crab, blue crabs are just as tasty. As you might guess, "she-crabs" are immature females of the species. For this elegant soup, however, you can use any form of crab. Fresh will have the most flavor, but frozen or canned are perfectly acceptable.

3 tablespoons unsalted butter

2 cups lump crabmeat, drained, picked over

1 hard-boiled egg yolk, pressed through a fine sieve

2 tablespoons grated onion

½ teaspoon Worcestershire sauce

3 cups half-and-half

1 tablespoon flour

2 tablespoons dry Sherry

Salt and freshly ground pepper to taste

2 tablespoons minced chives

Melt 2 tablespoons of the butter in a large bowl placed over simmering water. Add the crabmeat, egg yolk, grated onion and Worcestershire sauce.

In a medium-size pot placed over medium heat, bring the half-and-half almost to a boil. Rub together the remaining tablespoon of butter with the flour to form a paste. Drop, bit by bit, into the half-and-half. Whisk and heat until slightly thickened.

Pour the hot half-and-half over the crab mixture and gently fold. Add the Sherry, salt and pepper and gently simmer for 15 minutes. Ladle into individual bowls, sprinkle with the chives and serve.

Marilee's Fried Chicken

SERVES 4

TALK ABOUT THIS DISH anywhere in the South and emotions immediately get fired up over who makes "the best." It's a culinary institution, after all! Techniques and cooking methods vary with the cook, but surprisingly, fried chicken did not acquire its legendary status as a southern specialty until the early decades of the 20th century. Of all the recipes I've tasted, I still love my mother Marilee's version the best. Maybe it's the peanut oil she uses for frying, or maybe her trick of dipping the chicken pieces first in milk before dredging them in flour. Either way it's finger-licking good and everyone agrees that's the ONLY way to eat fried chicken.

1   3- to 5-pound chicken, cut into 8 pieces
    Peanut oil
1   cup flour
1   teaspoon salt
½   teaspoon freshly ground pepper
1   medium-large brown paper lunch bag
1   cup milk

Rinse the chicken and pat dry with paper towels.

Bring 1 inch of the oil to 360°F in a heavy, deep pot placed over medium-high heat.

Combine the flour, salt and pepper in the paper bag. Pour the milk into a large bowl. Working with 1 piece at a time, place the chicken in the paper bag and shake well. Remove the piece, dip it in the milk and then return it to the bag and shake again until it is coated with the flour mixture. Place each piece on a plate until all the pieces have been coated.

Put as many pieces as you can in the oil without crowding the pot. Fry, turning often as they brown, for 15 to 20 minutes. Repeat until all the chicken is fried. Serve immediately.

Ham and Red-Eye Gravy

SERVES 4

Pork is "poke" in the South, as indigenous a foodstuff as clams are to New England or salmon to the Northwest. It used to be that anyone with a farm had a pig, and ham, the succulent hind leg cut, provided a family's food all winter. Although that's rare today when huge agribusiness operations raise pigs on a mass scale, Southerners still love their ham. Premium Smithfield hams, dry-smoked and aged for a year, are considered the finest. Along with ham, red-eye gravy also checks in as a southern culinary legend, the best thing for breakfast when you wake up with a hangover. Add some eggs over easy and you're ready to take on the world!

4 tablespoons butter or bacon drippings

4 ¼-inch-thick slices country ham steaks

1 cup strong-brewed coffee

Melt the butter in a large, heavy skillet placed over low heat. Add the ham steaks and fry until the edges begin to brown, about 5 minutes. Turn the steaks over and brown on the other side. Add the brewed coffee, raise the heat to high and boil for 3 minutes. Remove the ham from the pan and keep in a warm place. Boil the gravy until it is slightly thick, loosening any browned bits from the bottom of the pan with a wooden spoon.

Pour the gravy over the ham steaks and serve.

Low Country Boil

LOW COUNTRY IN GEORGIA, OR ANYWHERE along the southeastern coast, refers to marshes and meadows that are below sea level or just barely above the tidal plain. Neighbors stick together in the towns and villages of this low-lying area, often gathering for cookouts where everyone contributes the bounty of their pantries or the catch of the day. Similar to a New England clambake in that these are events as much as occasions to eat, this spicy stew is always served. Often called Frogmore Stew, it originated with African-American families in the little town of Frogmore on St. Helena Island. When a boil is on, large pots bubble over backyard fires and crowds gather to feast at the outdoor party.

1 lemon, sliced

1 tablespoon Chesapeake seasoning (such as Old Bay or JO)

12 to 16 small new potatoes (about 3 pounds)

2 pounds kielbasa sausage, cut into 1-inch sections

2 medium onions, halved

4 ears corn on the cob, cut into 1-inch pieces

3 pounds large shrimp

Fill a large stock pot ⅓ full of water. Add the lemon slices, seasoning, potatoes and sausage. Bring to a boil over high heat. Lower the heat and simmer. After 20 minutes, add the onions and continue to cook for 10 more minutes. Add the corn and shrimp and cook until the shrimp are bright coral-colored, about 5 to 7 minutes.

Drain the contents of the pot and serve immediately.

13

Savannah

Pecan-Crusted Catfish

SERVES 6

CATFISH IS ANOTHER SOUTHERN CULINARY TRADITION, *especially the native channel catfish that roam the bays and eddys around Savannah's tidal coastline. Fairly easy to catch and always good eating, it's customary to dredge catfish fillets in flour and fry them to a golden brown. Cornmeal hush puppies and a big bowl of coleslaw complete the menu. For this recipe, adding toasted pecans to the crunchy cornmeal mixture adds an appealing nutty flavor to the crisp coating around the fish. By the way, pecans are the most important native nut in America and Georgia is where most are grown.*

1 cup pecan halves

6 6-ounce catfish fillets

1 cup buttermilk

2 eggs

1 teaspoon hot pepper sauce (such as Tabasco)

½ cup flour

½ cup yellow cornmeal

1 teaspoon salt

3 cups peanut oil

Lemon wedges for garnish

Preheat the oven to 400°F. Spread the pecans on a baking sheet and toast for 8 to 10 minutes. Remove and let them cool. Put the cooled pecans in the bowl of a food processor and pulse until they form a coarse meal. Don't let them become too buttery.

Rinse the catfish and pat dry with paper towels. In a wide, shallow bowl, whisk together the buttermilk, eggs and hot sauce. In another bowl, stir together the flour, cornmeal and salt. Bring the oil to 360°F in a large, heavy skillet placed over medium-high heat. Dip each fillet into the buttermilk mixture and then into the cornmeal mixture. Place on a piece of waxed paper until all the fillets are coated. Fry the fillets, a few at a time so as not to crowd the skillet, for about 5 minutes, until they are golden brown. Lift out with a slotted spatula and drain on paper towels while the remaining fish are fried.

Serve immediately with lemon wedges for garnish.

Fried Green Tomatoes

SERVES 4

Yes, there was a terrific movie with this name in the early 1990s, and before the movie, a book. Although this dish outdates either of those, its real origin is elusive. Maybe some enterprising southern cook, faced with the season's unripened tomatoes and being too frugal to toss them on the compost, decided to cook them instead. Fried foods being a southern tradition, it was natural to coat the bright green slices with cornmeal and slip them into a waiting pan of peanut oil. A legend was born! Remember never to cook tomatoes in an aluminum pan or they will lose their color and take on a bitter taste.

6 slices bacon, chopped

½ cup peanut oil

1 cup flour

1 cup yellow cornmeal

1 teaspoon salt

1 teaspoon freshly ground pepper

4 green tomatoes, sliced ½-inch thick

In a large, heavy skillet over medium-high heat, fry the bacon until crisp, about 5 minutes. Remove with a slotted spoon to paper towels and remove half of the bacon drippings. Add ¼ cup of the peanut oil.

In a wide, shallow bowl, combine the flour, cornmeal, salt and pepper. Return the skillet to medium-high heat. Dredge both sides of the tomato slices in the flour mixture and fry in batches, 3 to 5 minutes on each side, until they are all brown and crisp. Add the remaining oil as needed. Drain on paper towels.

Serve hot, topped with the crumbled bacon.

Candied Sweet Potatoes

SERVES 4

SMALL POTATOES IN THE SOUTH ARE LIKE dandelions in some folks' lawns. They're everywhere! They've been a staple of southern cooking since Native Americans first shared the wild variety with English colonists in Virginia who quickly figured out that they were worth cultivating. A fast grower, the sweet potato came into its own after that. Its naturally sweet, starchy, smooth orange flesh is an ingredient used in many traditional baked goods, from cakes and breads to waffles and biscuits. Here, candied sweet potatoes are a rich and delicious side dish made with butter, brown sugar and a hint of orange to enhance their taste.

4 medium sweet potatoes (about 1½ pounds)

½ cup unsalted butter, melted

1 cup brown sugar

¼ cup orange juice

Salt and freshly ground pepper to taste

Peel the sweet potatoes and cut into ½-inch slices. Combine the butter, brown sugar and orange juice in a large pan. Add the sweet potatoes and bring to a boil over high heat. Lower the heat to a simmer. Cover and cook for 30 minutes. If too much liquid evaporates, add a little water or more orange juice. After 30 minutes, remove the cover and cook until the liquid is syrupy and the potatoes are tender, about 5 to 10 minutes. Sprinkle with salt and pepper to taste.

Skillet Corn Bread

SERVES 8

CORN BREAD IS AN AMERICAN TRADITION *dating as far back as the Native Americans who grew maize as a staple and taught the first colonists how to make hoe cakes and jonnycakes. While every community has its corn bread variation, ranging from simple to more elaborate like the recipe here made with buttermilk and corn kernels, basic goodness is baked into each. Note that cornmeal in the South is whiter than that found in northern markets and, although not critical, some favor this style for a lighter end result. Use a traditional cast iron skillet to bake this bread, if you have one. The heavy pan heats slowly and contributes to a crisp outer surface.*

¼ cup corn oil

2 cups yellow cornmeal

½ cup flour

1 tablespoon sugar

1 tablespoon baking powder

1 teaspoon salt

½ teaspoon baking soda

2 cups buttermilk

2 eggs, lightly beaten

2 tablespoons unsalted butter, melted

2 cups fresh or frozen corn kernels

Preheat the oven to 450°F. Pour the corn oil into a heavy skillet and tip it so the oil coats its sides. Place the skillet in the oven until it becomes very hot, about 5 minutes. Remove from the oven and pour off any excess oil.

In a medium-size mixing bowl, combine the cornmeal, flour, sugar, baking powder, salt and baking soda. Stir in the buttermilk, eggs and butter until just mixed. Fold in the corn kernels. Pour the batter into the skillet and place in the oven. Reduce the temperature to 400°F and bake for 25 minutes, until the bread is lightly browned around the edges and is pulling from the sides of the skillet.

Applesauce Cake

APPLE SEEDS WERE BROUGHT TO THE NEW WORLD by the first colonists to start domestic apple orchards. Apple varieties found in America today are a distinct species with only a few characteristics that overlap with their European cousins. This appealing cake has its own heritage of spices and nuts, ingredients that traditionally were saved to use when cooking for special occasions. The bourbon-flavored frosting is pure southern style and adds a nip of flavor to this delightful cake.

CAKE

- 3½ cups sifted flour
- 1 teaspoon baking soda
- 2 teaspoons ground nutmeg
- 1 teaspoon ground cinnamon
- ½ teaspoon ground cloves
- 1 cup sugar
- 1 cup chopped walnuts
- 1 cup light raisins
- 1 cup unsalted butter, room temperature
- 2 eggs
- 16 ounces applesauce

FROSTING

- ¾ cup unsalted butter, softened
- 1 tablespoon heavy cream
- 4 cups confectioner's sugar (1 pound)
- Pinch salt
- 2 tablespoons bourbon
- 2 tablespoons apple cider or juice

FOR CAKE: Preheat the oven to 350°F. Coat a 10-inch tube pan with butter.

Sift the flour, baking soda, nutmeg, cinnamon, cloves and sugar into a large mixing bowl. In another bowl, combine the walnuts and raisins and toss them with half of the flour mixture.

Beat the butter until it is fluffy, about 3 to 5 minutes. Add the eggs, one at a time. Alternately add the flour mixture and the applesauce to the butter, beginning and ending with the flour. Stir in the raisin mixture. Pour the batter into the prepared pan and bake for 1 hour and 20 minutes, until a cake tester comes out clean. Cool the cake on a metal rack for 15 minutes. Turn out to finish cooling.

FOR FROSTING: Beat the butter and cream together in a bowl with an electric mixer set on low speed. Add 1 cup of the confectioner's sugar and the salt. Gradually add the remaining sugar, the bourbon and apple cider and beat until the mixture is smooth. Top the cake with the frosting.

Martha Nesbit's Peach Pound Cake

SERVES 8 TO 10

IF YOU WANT TO LEARN ABOUT Savannah's proud history, you should have the good fortune to meet Martha Nesbit, as I did on my visit to this glorious coastal city. Not only is she an award-winning journalist who served many years as food and lifestyle editor for the city's newspaper, as well as writing a book about Savannah's rich heritage, she's also a gracious hostess who knows how to give a party in true southern style. Her recipe here celebrates Georgia's famous peaches in a show-stopping tube cake drizzled with a distinctive fresh lemon glaze.

CAKE

Nonstick cooking spray

3 cups plus 2 tablespoons sifted all-purpose flour

1 cup unsalted butter, softened

3 cups sugar

6 large eggs

1 cup sour cream

1 teaspoon vanilla extract

1 teaspoon almond extract

½ teaspoon baking soda

2 cups peeled chopped drained peaches

GLAZE

1½ cups confectioner's sugar

4 tablespoons fresh lemon juice

1 teaspoon almond extract

1 peach, thinly sliced

Juice of 1 lemon

Fresh blackberries for garnish

FOR CAKE: Preheat the oven to 325°F. Coat a 10-inch tube pan with nonstick cooking spray. Add the 2 tablespoons of flour and shake the pan to coat the insides.

Cream the butter and sugar for 5 minutes in a bowl with an electric mixer set on medium speed. Scrape down the sides and beat in the eggs and sour cream. Add the vanilla and almond extracts.

Sift the 3 cups of flour and the baking soda into a medium-size mixing bowl. Slowly add the flour to the butter mixture. Do not overmix. Fold in the peaches with a spatula. Pour the batter into the prepared pan.

Bake the cake on the bottom third of the oven for 1 hour and 25 minutes, or until a tester inserted in the center comes out clean.

Allow the cake to cool on a metal rack for 15 minutes, then, using a knife, loosen the cake from the sides of the pan, and then loosen the inner tube portion. Invert the cake onto a plate and then flip it back right side up onto a cake plate.

FOR GLAZE: Combine the confectioner's sugar, lemon juice and almond extract with a whisk in a small bowl. When it is very smooth, drizzle the glaze over the top of the cake. Right before serving, decorate with fresh sliced peaches that have been dipped in the lemon juice and fresh blackberries.

Florida Keys

Fried Calamari with Raisin Chutney

Jerked Chicken with Mango Salsa

Conch Fritters

Caribbean Black Bean Salad

Pulled Pork

Coconut Spoon Bread

Broiled Red Snapper with Rum Butter

Key Lime Pie

The best way to discover the Florida Keys is to drive down U.S. Route 1. It's a two-lane concrete ribbon of highway and bridges that leapfrogs 110 miles down a chain of mangrove-fringed islands dangling west-southwest from the tip of the mainland. On the right side are the silvery blue-green Florida Bay and Gulf of Mexico and on the left is the vast Atlantic Ocean. On both sides are breathtaking sweeps of shimmering sea and endless sky.

I drove this highway through the expected assortment of tourist traps that line the main road. But I knew that all around were living coral reefs, coconut palms, lagoons, terrific fishing, snorkeling and diving, plus some of the planet's most gorgeous sunsets. These, plus an air of sultry intrigue and romance, and a history of swashbuckling misfits and colorful characters, lure refugees from all over.

Key West lies at the end of the Florida Keys. Sitting on the edge of the Caribbean and just 90 miles from Havana, it's always been a bit exotic with a laid-back, nonconformist lifestyle. That's true of its culinary style, too. Now a small city, it's a vibrant place with ginger-bread Victorian houses, museums, slightly seedy watering holes, dozens of galleries, bed and breakfast inns, and restaurants that have been spruced up and renovated over the past ten years as tourism has boomed.

Would you believe Key West was once the richest town in the U.S. and the largest settlement in Florida? Salvage operations from wrecked ships that ran aground on the reefs, and shrimp, pineapple, and natural sponge businesses all thrived here before the Depression and hurricanes blew them away and tourism took over. Key West was an important Navy port, too, during WWII and the Korean War. With all the characters that have lived in this town over the years, no wonder Ernest Hemingway and President Harry Truman liked to hang out here.

But I like to eat and that was my motivation for visiting these islands. They are a mecca now for some very innovative cooking. Yes, you may find the occasional 'gator' steak on a restaurant menu since the Everglades aren't that far away, but Caribbean immigrants have added their sizzling food traditions. The result is a tantalizing form of fusion cuisine that features fresh seafood, Florida's abundant citrus and tropical fruit and Caribbean spices and fiery rubs.

Among the specialties of the Keys are conch fritters and key lime pie. The crispy deep-fried fritters are so named for the creature that lives inside a beautiful curled shell found only in the waters off the Keys and the Caribbean islands. Real key lime pie is worth going out of your way for since this delicately flavored treat tastes like nothing else on earth.

The other recipes I've selected here will give you a more complete sampling of cooking in the Keys. Just imagine lapping waves, a gorgeous sunset and you'll have the perfect atmos-phere for a tropical island feast.

Fried Calamari with Raisin Chutney

SERVES 8

THE CARIBBEAN IS A CROSSROADS OF cultures. East Indians in the British Empire migrated to posts in the West Indies and generations later, their culinary traditions are part of what's considered native cuisine. Since fried and well-seasoned foods are beloved throughout the islands, this dish qualifies as a hands-down favorite. The sweet and sour taste of the fruit-based chutney paired with crispy, golden calamari rings is terrific—tasty and with great texture.

¼ cup golden raisins

¼ cup white rum

¼ cup brown sugar

2 green onions, sliced

¼ cup cider vinegar

3 tablespoons lime juice

¼ teaspoon allspice

¼ teaspoon ground cinnamon

¼ teaspoon ground nutmeg or freshly grated

¼ teaspoon salt

1 teaspoon finely diced gingerroot

1 mango, diced

1 banana, diced

1 quart corn oil

4 pounds calamari, cleaned

2 12-ounce cans beer

2½ cups flour

2 teaspoons baking powder

1 teaspoon salt

Soak the raisins in the rum for 30 minutes in a small bowl. In a heavy pot, combine the brown sugar, green onions, cider vinegar, lime juice, allspice, cinnamon, nutmeg, ¼ teaspoon salt, ginger, mango and banana. Bring to a simmer over medium heat. Stir constantly and cook until the chutney thickens, about 5 minutes. Remove to a bowl. When cooled, cover and refrigerate until ready to serve.

Bring 3 inches of corn oil in a deep pot to 400°F over low heat. Preheat the oven to 500°F.

Rinse and pat dry the calamari. Cut into ½-inch rings. In a medium-size bowl, whisk together the beer, flour, baking powder and 1 teaspoon salt. Dunk the rings in the batter, allowing the excess to drip back into the bowl. Fry 3 to 5 rings at a time. Be sure not to crowd the pan. Cook for about 1 minute, turning once to brown both sides. Remove from the oil with a slotted spoon and drain on paper towels placed on a baking sheet.

When all of the rings have been fried, remove the paper towels from the baking sheet and crisp the calamari in the hot oven for 3 minutes. Serve immediately with the chutney.

Conch Fritters

THERE'S NO DOUBT YOU'RE IN the Caribbean when you find conch on the menu. It's a large, single-shelled mollusk that lives much like a snail in tropical waters. A conch will have been removed from its shell and cleaned before sale. Conch fritters in one form or another, served with a choice of sauces, are a popular appetizer all around the islands.

- 1 pound conch, removed from shell, cut into small pieces
- 1 cup flour
- 1 teaspoon baking powder
- 1 egg
- ½ cup milk
- 2 garlic cloves, minced
- 1 jalapeño pepper, seeded, minced
- ¼ cup fresh lime juice
- 1 tablespoon Worcestershire sauce
- 4 drops hot pepper sauce (such as Tabasco)
- 1 quart corn oil
- Lime wedges
- Salsa

Rinse and pat dry the conch. Place in a food processor and pulse until it is finely ground. In a medium-size mixing bowl, sift the flour and baking powder together. Add the conch, egg, milk, garlic, jalapeño, lime juice, Worcestershire and hot sauce. Blend well and let rest for 5 minutes.

Bring the corn oil to 375°F in a deep, heavy pot over medium heat. Preheat the oven to 200°F. Drop 5 to 7 teaspoonfuls of batter (or heaping tablespoons if used as an entrée) into the oil and cook for 2 minutes (3 minutes per side for large fritters). Turn to brown the other side for 2 minutes. Remove with a slotted spoon to paper towels placed on a baking sheet. Keep warm in the oven while cooking the remaining batter.

Serve hot with lime wedges or salsa.

Pulled Pork

SERVES 12 TO 15

HIGHLY SEASONED RUBS AND PASTES are common in Caribbean cooking as the popularity of jerked foods testifies. This oven-cooked variation uses traditional pork that's slow-cooked Jamaican-style until the meat is so tender it practically melts in your mouth. Slow-cooking, a traditional cooking method of free Africans and slaves in Jamaica, made inexpensive meats more savory. The creative use of spices is pure Caribbean—intense and a bit exotic—borrowed from the French and Spanish. Served sandwich-style on buns, it's also pure American.

2 4- to 5-pound boneless pork butts

4 onions, chopped

2 tablespoons dried thyme

2 tablespoons salt

1 tablespoon allspice

¼ teaspoon ground nutmeg or freshly grated

¼ teaspoon ground cinnamon

1 tablespoon freshly ground pepper

6 garlic cloves

1 cup cider vinegar

½ cup water

2 tablespoons Worcestershire sauce

1 tablespoon freshly ground pepper

1 tablespoon salt

2 teaspoons vegetable oil

Place the pork butts, fat side up, on a cutting board and slice each in half. In a food processor, puree the onions, thyme, 2 tablespoons salt, allspice, nutmeg, cinnamon, pepper and garlic until the mixture forms a paste. Rub the paste all over the pieces of pork. Cover and refrigerate for 2 to 24 hours.

Preheat the oven to 225°F. Place the pork butts on a rack set in a deep roasting pan. In a small bowl, combine the cider vinegar, water, Worcestershire sauce, pepper, 1 tablespoon salt and vegetable oil. Using a wide brush, mop the pork with the mixture. Place in the oven. Mop every 30 minutes for about 6 hours, until the internal temperature reaches 165°F. Be sure to use all of the sauce.

Remove the pork from the oven and set aside until it is cool enough to handle. At that point, shred or chop the tender pork. Serve on or with soft buns. Spoon each mound of pork with pan drippings.

Broiled Red Snapper with Rum Butter

SERVES 4

A DAYLONG OCEAN-FISHING TRIP GAVE ME new respect for this rosy-colored, medium-sized fish that's common in the Gulf of Mexico. Although there are several species of this fish almost everywhere around the world, red snapper is most closely identified with Florida cuisine. No doubt that's because it's abundant and a favorite with the Sunshine State's chefs and customers alike who enjoy its flaky white meat and delicate taste. Try it here with unexpected spices and a hint of rum flavoring for an entirely different taste sensation.

4 tablespoons unsalted butter, softened

1 tablespoon minced fresh chives

½ cup dark rum

4 8-ounce red snapper fillets

1 garlic clove, minced

1 teaspoon dried thyme

½ teaspoon allspice

¼ teaspoon ground nutmeg or freshly grated

¼ teaspoon ground cinnamon

¼ teaspoon salt

¼ teaspoon cayenne pepper

Blend the butter, chives and ⅓ cup of the rum in a small bowl using a rubber spatula. Place a 10-inch sheet of plastic wrap on a smooth surface. Scrape the butter mixture along the nearest edge of the sheet, leaving a few inches on either end for twisting. Roll up the butter to form a 1-inch-thick log. Twist the ends, fold under to seal and place in the refrigerator for 2 hours.

Preheat the broiler. Rinse and pat dry the fillets. Coat the bottom of a 11 x 9 x 2-inch pan with butter. Arrange the fillets, skin side down, in the pan so they do not touch. In a small bowl, combine the garlic, thyme, allspice, nutmeg, cinnamon, salt and cayenne pepper. Sprinkle the fish with the seasonings and drizzle with the remaining rum.

While the fish is cooking, cut the rum butter into 4 rounds. Place the fish 4 inches under the broiler. Cook the fish for 5 to 7 minutes, until it is opaque and flakes easily. Carefully lift out each fillet, using a large, metal spatula, and place on dinner plates. Top each fillet with a piece of the compound butter. Spoon the hot juice from the pan over the butter and fish. Serve immediately.

Jerked Chicken with Mango Salsa

THE CARIBBEAN ISLAND OF JAMAICA is the homeland of jerked meats, a fiery type of barbecue preparation that uses a spice and pepper-encrusted, slow-smoked cooking process called "jerk." Maroons, escaped slaves living in the island's jungle interior in the 18th century, developed the process to prepare their favorite food, wild boar or pork. Its unique smoky flavor is derived from the wood of the pimento tree. There's a mystique about jerk sauces and every island cook has their own recipe.

1	onion, diced
½	teaspoon thyme
2	teaspoons molasses
1	teaspoon allspice
½	teaspoon ground cinnamon
1	jalapeño pepper, seeded, diced
3	tablespoons soy sauce
1	tablespoon corn oil
1	tablespoon white vinegar
2	3-pound chickens, cut into serving-size pieces
2	mangos, cut into small dice
1	teaspoon minced gingerroot
1	jalapeño pepper, seeded, finely diced
½	red bell pepper, seeded, diced
2	green onions, sliced
2	garlic cloves, minced
2	tablespoons extra-virgin olive oil
1	tablespoon white vinegar
2	tablespoons chopped fresh cilantro

Place the onion, thyme, molasses, allspice, cinnamon, jalapeño, soy sauce, corn oil and white vinegar in the bowl of a food processor. Process until the mixture is smooth.

Rub the chickens with the marinade and place in a large pan. Cover and refrigerate for 4 hours. While the chickens are marinating, prepare the mango salsa. Combine the mangos, ginger, jalapeño, red pepper, green onions, garlic, olive oil, white vinegar and cilantro in a small mixing bowl. Cover and refrigerate until the chicken is cooked.

Bring the grill to medium heat. Add a handful of hickory or apple wood chips, soaked in beer, to the fire. Place the chicken on the grill, skin side down, cover and cook for 15 minutes. Open the lid and baste with the extra marinade left in the pan and turn the pieces over. Cover the grill and cook for another 10 to 15 minutes. Serve the chicken with a small mound of mango salsa.

Caribbean Black Bean Salad

SERVES 6 TO 8

BLACK BEANS, OR TURTLE BEANS, ARE the beans of choice all around the Caribbean. They are earthy, flavorful, somewhat more assertive tasting than other beans, and a source of protein for agricultural island cultures. The unusual combination here of cooked bacon, fragrant spices, diced red and jalapeño peppers, lime juice and green onions, gives this salad its festival of zesty flavors and implies its African origins. I like to make it ahead and serve it with chicken dishes.

2   13-ounce cans black beans, drained, rinsed

3   slices bacon, diced

2   tablespoons peanut oil

1   medium onion, diced

1   teaspoon dried thyme

1   teaspoon allspice

¼   teaspoon ground nutmeg or freshly grated

½   teaspoon ground cinnamon

2   jalapeño peppers, seeded, diced

1   red bell pepper, seeded, diced

4   green onions, sliced

Juice of 2 limes

½   teaspoon salt

Place the black beans in a large mixing bowl and set aside.

In a heavy skillet over medium heat, cook the bacon in the peanut oil until it begins to brown, about 3 to 5 minutes. Add the onion and cook for 5 minutes. Stir in the thyme, allspice, nutmeg and cinnamon and cook for another 3 minutes.

Pour the onion mixture over the beans. Add the jalapeños, red bell pepper, green onions, lime juice and salt. Toss well. Cover and chill for 1 hour. Toss once more before serving.

Coconut Spoon Bread

SERVES 6

THERE ARE ALMOST AS MANY *"authentic" recipes for spoon bread in the South as there are cooks. What makes it genuine is the subject of constant discussion, but it's usually made with white cornmeal, eggs, butter and milk, and baked on a griddle or in a greased pan. In honor of Key West's beautiful coconut palms, I've adapted a fairly standard recipe to use coconut cream. You can usually buy canned coconut cream in the Asian foods section of your supermarket.*

3½ cups milk
½ cup coconut cream
1 cup cornmeal
3 eggs, beaten
2 tablespoons unsalted butter, melted
1 teaspoon salt

Preheat the oven to 425°F.

In large, heavy pot over low heat, warm 3 cups of the cream. In a medium-size bowl, place the remaining milk and the coconut cream and then stir in the cornmeal. Slowly stir the cornmeal mixture into the heated milk. Stir constantly for 5 minutes. Remove from the heat and stir in the eggs, butter and salt. Pour into an 11 x 9 x 2-inch baking pan. Bake for 45 minutes.

Remove from the oven and let rest on a metal rack for 5 minutes. Cut into squares and serve warm.

Key Lime Pie

SERVES 6

TRUE KEY LIME PIE IS A world-famous Florida delicacy, often imitated, but never duplicated, with domestic limes. The first Key limes came to the Florida Keys almost 150 years ago from Mexico where they had been introduced by Spanish explorers. They were grown commercially in the Keys before severe storms in 1926 destroyed most of the groves. Some groves are returning today, but real Key lime aficionados search for wild trees. Rarely shipped out of state, this lime is a golden shade when ripe and smaller than its hybrid cousin, the Persian lime, offering a certain subtle and wild tang. If no Key limes are available, use bottled Key lime juice, found in most specialty markets.

1   9-inch prepared pie shell

2   cups heavy cream

1   14-ounce can sweetened
    condensed milk

½   cup Key lime juice (if available) or
    lime juice

1   tablespoon minced Key lime zest
    (if available) or lime zest

¼   teaspoon salt

Bake the prepared pie shell according to the directions on its package. Set aside to cool.

Beat 1 cup of the heavy cream in the bowl of an electric mixer until stiff. In a large mixing bowl, whisk together the sweetened condensed milk, Key lime juice, zest and salt. Gently fold in the whipped cream. Pour into the cooled pie shell. Refrigerate for 3 hours.

Just before serving, beat the remaining cream with the electric mixer until stiff. Using a pastry bag fitted with a star tip, pipe the whipped cream onto the chilled pie.

SOUTHWEST

Head for the American Southwest, whether Texas, Arizona or New Mexico, and you find that the sky stretches out, the hills become angular and gold-colored, and cottonwood and willow trees hug the arroyos in search of water and are just as rangy as the cattle that roam the ranches here. In this part of the country there are also hot, dry deserts, as well as plateaus, piney woods, plains, prairies and bayous, along with the mighty Rio Grande that intersects the entire region on its way to the Gulf of Mexico. I quickly discovered that with all its different geographies, the Southwest is a rich historical intersection of cultures, and many of these cultural traditions involve food. As a result, southwestern cuisine is diverse and delicious, down-home and no-frills, as well as sophisticated, fiery and complex.

First there were Native Americans who established sophisticated farming communities along fertile riverbeds and in rocky cliff dwellings, as well as more nomadic communities living on the plains and prairies. Then came the era of French and Spanish explorers who journeyed into the area from the Gulf Coast of Texas. The French claimed the Louisiana Territory, or all the land between the Appalachians and east of the Rio Grande. Missionaries followed them and more Spaniards pushed north from Mexico settling the vast frontier west of the Rio Grande. Where the new settlers crossed Native American lands, conflicts arose. Battles raged off and on for years as each side claimed the territory.

With so much cross-cultural interaction over the centuries, I wasn't surprised to discover how much the traditions of Spanish, Mexican and even Native American cuisines and ingredients overlap in the classic dishes of the Southwest. For example, Native Americans introduced European settlers to corn, beans and squash—vegetables that they'd grown for generations. In turn, Spanish colonists brought chili peppers—today the heart and soul of southwestern cooking—from Central America, as well as sugar, eggs and dairy cattle from Europe. These ingredients then inspired dishes using cheese and egg whites. Spices and herbs like cumin, cilantro, oregano and lemon thyme, and unusual fruits like tomatillos, all originating in Mexico, are seasonings that cooks from each culture experimented with in dishes that today are considered southwestern classics.

Just as various ethnic traditions mingled in the kitchens of the Southwest, I learned there's also a strong Tex-Mex culinary tradition in the border towns between the U.S. and Mexico. Here ingredients and flavors from both Texas and Mexico blend in tortillas, refried beans, tamales and enchiladas. You'll find examples of this cultural overlap in the names of some southwestern dishes: *chili con carne* is Spanish for "meat cooked with chiles" while jicama is a Mexican word for "yam bean" or, a crisp, white, edible tuber.

But whatever their origins, I think you'll agree that these dishes are all downright delicious. Some, like the Three Cheese and Vegetable Quesadillas and Refried Beans may be familiar, but others such as Picadillo, Calabacitas and Rompope Canela Helado may offer new taste sensations and send you back for second helpings.

Guacamole Boudro's

MAKES ABOUT 3 CUPS

WHO WOULD GUESS THIS BUTTERY, *slightly tangy condiment has been around since the days of the Aztecs? Despite the rather forbidding exterior of the avocado, this ancient culture discovered a good thing in the creamy, bright green flesh inside and we're all the luckier. In my exploration of San Antonio's favorite foods, I discovered this signature guacamole at Boudro's, a Texas-style bistro midway along the city's charming Riverwalk. To ensure the best results, be sure your avocados are ripe. They should give just a little around the stem area when gently pressed with your fingertips. You can hasten the ripening process by putting avocados in a closed plastic bag with a banana peel. (Yes, it really works.)*

4 ripe avocados, peeled, cut into ½-inch dice

½ teaspoon salt

Juice of 1 lime

Juice of 1 orange

1 large Roma tomato, diced

1 to 2 teaspoons serrano pepper, seeded, diced

2 teaspoons minced red onion

1 teaspoon minced fresh cilantro

Gently combine all of the ingredients in a medium-size serving bowl. Serve with tortilla chips.

Salsa Verde

TOMATILLOS ARE SUCH A CURIOUS fruit wrapped in their thin, brown paper husks. Similar to tiny green tomatoes, they have been used in Mexican cooking since ancient days when the Aztec and Mayan cultures flourished. The fruit has pale yellow or green flesh that's crisp, acidic and usually contains tiny seeds. If you want to use fresh tomatillas to make this zesty green salsa, first peel off the papery husks and roast them for about 7 minutes in a very hot oven on a baking sheet. Or cook them, husks removed, for a few minutes in boiling water to bring out the best flavor.

½ small onion, finely chopped

1 serrano or jalapeño pepper, seeded, finely chopped

10 to 12 ounces canned tomatillos, drained, coarsely chopped

1 tablespoon minced fresh cilantro

½ teaspoon salt

Freshly ground pepper to taste

Place all of the ingredients in a serving bowl and mix together well. For a smooth salsa, place all of the ingredients in the bowl of a food processor and puree.

Chicken Tortilla Soup

We gringos aren't the only ones with chicken soup on our list of comfort foods. Steaming pots of the golden broth were prepared in kitchens in south central Texas long ago—probably a century before the first Texas border even existed. So in San Antonio this classic dish brimming with chunks of chicken and a handful of vegetables has a decidedly Mexican flair from chili peppers and lime juice. The presence of tortillas, the major bread form of the New World made from corn or hominy (dried corn with the hulls removed), adds to this version's south-of-the-border character.

3½ cups chicken broth

1 pasilla or jalapeño pepper, halved

2 teaspoons olive oil

4 8- or 10-inch corn tortillas, cut into ½-inch strips

1 small onion, diced

½ stalk celery, diced

6 to 8 ounces cooked chicken, shredded

3 tablespoons fresh lime juice

Salt and freshly ground pepper to taste

Bring the chicken broth to a boil over high heat in a medium-size pot. Add the pepper, cover and remove from the heat. Let stand for 30 minutes. Strain the broth and set aside. Remove the seeds and stem from the pepper and finely chop. Set aside in a small bowl to use as garnish.

Heat the oil in the pot over medium heat. Add the tortilla strips and sauté until golden brown, about 3 to 5 minutes. Remove with a slotted spatula to drain on paper towels. Reduce the heat to low and add the onion and celery. Add a little more oil if necessary. Sauté for 5 to 7 minutes, until the onion is soft and the celery bright green. Add the chicken broth and raise the heat to medium. Simmer for 10 minutes. Add the chicken meat and lime juice. Season with the salt and pepper to taste and simmer for 5 minutes.

Place the tortilla strips in the bottom of each bowl. Top with the hot soup and garnish with the reserved chopped pepper.

Picadillo

THIS SAVORY STUFFING THAT HAS a bit of zing from jalapeño peppers is essentially a ground meat relish or hash that's used in traditional Mexican dishes like chiles relleños, directly translated as "stuffed peppers." It's often served with rice and bean dishes as well, because the zesty flavors of garlic, onion and red wine vinegar paired with sweet undercurrents of cinnamon, tomato paste and raisins complement these milder foods so well. My family especially loves it used as a satisfying quesadilla filling sprinkled with mild Monterey Jack cheese and sandwiched between corn or flour tortillas.

½ pound ground beef

½ pound ground pork

2 tablespoons red wine vinegar

Salt and freshly ground pepper to taste

1 small onion, minced

2   garlic cloves, minced

1 jalapeño pepper, seeded, minced

1 tablespoon olive oil

1 pound tomatoes, peeled, chopped

⅓ cup raisins

½ cup slivered almonds

½ teaspoon ground cloves

1 teaspoon ground cinnamon

2 tablespoons tomato paste

Wrappers (such as tortillas or tacos)

In a small bowl, mix together the beef, pork, vinegar, salt and pepper. Set aside.

In a large, heavy skillet placed over medium heat, sauté the onion, garlic and jalapeño in the olive oil for 3 to 5 minutes, until the onion starts to become clear. Raise the heat to medium-high and add the meat mixture. Break up the meat with a spoon and cook until it begins to brown, about 5 minutes. Drain off any fat and stir in the tomatoes, raisins, almonds, cloves, cinnamon and tomato paste. Simmer for 10 minutes.

Spoon into the desired wrapper.

Red Snapper Vera Cruz

SERVES 6

A FISH NATIVE TO THE GULF of Mexico, red snapper is appropriately named for its lovely red color and is prized throughout the southern United States and eastern Mexico for its flaky, mild-tasting white flesh that easily adapts to many preparations. My version here with tomatoes (canned are acceptable) accented by garlic, salty olives and capers and simply spiced with salt and crushed peppercorns is fresh-tasting and delicious. Named for the Mexican Gulf port city of Vera Cruz, it reflects the Spanish/ Mediterranean influence on Mexican cooking. Add a basket of fresh corn tortillas, white rice and refried beans, and you'll feast like a compadre.

1	onion, diced
4	garlic cloves, minced
3	tablespoons olive oil
1	pound tomatoes, peeled, seeded, diced
10	green olives, pitted, chopped
2	tablespoons drained capers
2	bay leaves
6	black peppercorns, crushed
	Salt to taste
2	pounds red snapper fillets, scaled
2	tablespoons minced fresh cilantro

Sauté the onion and garlic in 1 tablespoon of the olive oil in a large pot over low heat. When the onion begins to become clear, after about 3 to 5 minutes, stir in the tomatoes, olives, capers, bay leaves, peppercorns and salt. Raise the heat until it simmers and cook for 10 minutes.

Rub the snapper with the remaining 2 tablespoons of olive oil. Place a large skillet over medium-high heat and add the fish. Sprinkle with a little salt. Pour the sauce over the fish and bring to a boil. Reduce the heat until the sauce simmers, cover and cook for 8 minutes, until the fish becomes opaque.

Serve the snapper, covered with the sauce and garnished with the fresh cilantro.

Three-Cheese and Vegetable Quesadillas

SERVES 6

I CLAIM QUESADILLAS ARE TEX-MEX fast food at its finest. Fast to prepare and satisfying to eat, these crispy tortilla pockets filled with melted cheese and any number of ingredients can be simple or sophisticated. Borrowed from a classic Mexican recipe, quesadillas are to Latinos like sandwiches are to us. Happily, we've discovered how good they are and how easy to make, so we've adopted quesadillas with equal pleasure. To make this garden vegetable version, use fresh flour or corn tortillas and don't leave out the cilantro.

¼ cup shredded Monterey Jack cheese

¼ cup shredded Cheddar cheese

2 tablespoons crumbled feta cheese

1 jalapeño pepper, seeded, diced

2 garlic cloves, minced

½ medium tomato, diced

1 green onion, sliced

½ medium zucchini, diced

1 teaspoon olive oil

2 tablespoons chopped fresh cilantro

6 10-inch tortillas

Cilantro sprigs for garnish

In a small bowl, toss together all of the cheeses.

In a medium-size skillet placed over medium heat, sauté the jalapeño pepper, garlic, tomato, green onion and zucchini in the olive oil for 2 to 3 minutes. Gently stir in the cilantro. Remove from the heat and set aside.

Lay a tortilla in a medium-size skillet placed over medium heat and spread with 2 tablespoons of the cheeses and 2 tablespoons of the vegetable mixture. Fold the tortilla in half and cook each side for 1 to 2 minutes, until the cheeses begin to melt. Lift out of the skillet and keep warm as the remaining quesadillas are prepared.

Serve each quesadilla garnished with the cilantro sprigs.

Pecos River Red Chili

SERVES 6

THE PECOS RIVER WANDERS DOWN through southwest Texas and at the Mexican border joins the Rio Grande on its way to the Gulf. Out here in ranch country, they like their chili hot and no-nonsense, which in Texas means no beans. In fact, chili con carne—Spanish for "chili peppers with meat," is traditionally made in Texas without beans, at least if the dish claims to be authentic Texas chili. While there is some room for discussion, "true believers" will not argue about the ingredients. The only thing debatable is what degree of fire power makes a chili worthy of its name. My advice is to taste before adding all the chili powder at once, and serve beans on the side, Texas-style.

1½ pounds lean ground beef

2 garlic cloves, chopped

1 tablespoon hot chili powder

2 teaspoons mild chili powder

2 teaspoons ground cumin

½ large onion, chopped

1 tablespoon bacon fat

1 teaspoon salt

1 teaspoon paprika

1½ cups water

In a medium-size bowl, combine the beef, garlic, chili powders and cumin. In a large skillet placed over medium-high heat, sauté the onion in the bacon fat for 3 minutes. Add the meat mixture, salt and paprika and cook for about 15 minutes, until the meat is browned. Break up the meat as it cooks. Add the water and lower the heat until the chili just simmers. Cover and cook for 30 minutes, or until the meat is tender. Serve over rice.

Refried Beans

BEANS ARE A STAPLE IN NORTHERN MEXICO *and throughout the Southwest where they have long provided an important source of protein. As cuisines mingled over the centuries in this part of the world, beans turn up in Spanish, Mexican, Texan and New Mexican dishes paired with corn in a healthful and delicious combination. Interestingly, "refried" as it's translated from the Spanish "refritos" does not mean "fried again." Instead, "re" with "fritos" is used for emphasis to mean "well-fried" or "intensely fried" until the previously boiled beans are almost dry, but rich and satisfying.*

3 garlic cloves, minced

1 small onion, finely chopped

3 tablespoons bacon fat

4 cups cooked pinto beans

Salt to taste

¾ cup grated Monterey Jack cheese

Sauté the garlic and onion with the bacon fat in a large skillet placed over low heat. When the garlic begins to brown, after about 3 to 5 minutes, add the beans. Mash the beans with the back of a spoon or with a potato masher. Add some water, a few tablespoons at a time, until the bean mixture is slightly soupy. Raise the heat to medium and simmer for 20 minutes, until the beans are thick and slightly crispy around the edges. Adjust the flavor with salt and serve topped with the cheese.

Calabacitas

This dish is named after the light green, round or pear-shaped Mexican squash that's related to our zucchini. Since it's tender-skinned, it doesn't travel well and is rarely found in American markets unless it is in a specialty vegetable or ethnic market. Zucchini is a good substitute for this vegetable side dish that's traditional throughout the Southwest. Fresh corn is an integral ingredient, and the dish is almost always served with a spoonful of sour cream or a sprinkling of goat cheese and pepitas (toasted sunflower or pumpkin seeds).

½ onion, diced

3 tablespoons corn oil

2 poblano peppers, seeded, diced

1 cup fresh corn kernels

1 pound zucchini, cut into ½-inch cubes

Salt to taste

Sauté the onion in the corn oil for 3 minutes in a large, heavy skillet placed over medium heat. Add the peppers and corn kernels and cook for 3 more minutes. Stir in the zucchini cubes and cook until they are slightly browned, about 5 to 7 minutes. Season with salt and serve.

Rompope-Canela Helado

MAKES 1 QUART

WHEN THE SPANISH ARRIVED IN MEXICO, they brought with them dairy ingredients like milk and cream, which along with eggs, sugar and cinnamon, made a perfect match for vanilla, a Mexican original. All are ideal ingredients for ice cream and flan, Mexico's "official" dessert and a favorite in San Antonio, too. But to prove that there's something other than flan on the dessert list in Texas, try this delectable, sophisticated version of a very custardy ice cream. Look for canela, the flowery scented cinnamon grown in Southeast Asia, but widely used in Mexico, in specialty food markets for a subtle, authentic taste.

¾ cup sugar

2 teaspoons cornstarch

2 teaspoons ground cinnamon or canela (if available)

Pinch salt

2 eggs

4 egg yolks

2½ cups milk

½ cup heavy cream

2 teaspoons brandy

½ teaspoon vanilla extract

In a large, heavy pot, whisk together the sugar, cornstarch, cinnamon and salt. Beat in the eggs, yolks, milk and cream. Place over medium-low heat and stir constantly for 20 minutes, until the mixture begins to thicken. Do not let it boil or the eggs will scramble.

Stir in the brandy and vanilla extract and remove from the heat. Pour through a fine sieve into a large bowl and allow to cool. Process in an ice cream maker according to the manufacturer's directions.

New Orleans

Beignets

Shrimp Jambalaya

Boudin Balls

Red Beans and Rice

Spicy Fried Shrimp Remoulade

Butter Beans

Crab and Crawfish Cardinal

Raisin Cake with Rum Sauce

Filé Gumbo

Praline Sundae

$\mathcal{F}$orget jazz and zydeco. Forget Mardi Gras, the French Quarter with its graceful wrought iron balconies dripping bougainvillea, Bourbon Street and Old Man River with its paddle wheelers and barges. What you really need to do when you come to New Orleans is eat! I don't think you can be here five minutes before you realize New Orleans residents are passionate about food. Everywhere in this seductive city of semi-tropical heat and humidity along the mighty Mississippi tempting aromas waft out of restaurants and homes. Some say the natives are obsessive about food here and you might agree when you learn the entire city eats only red beans and rice on Mondays.

New Orleans' culinary traditions have their roots in the city's colorful history. It is French and Spanish, black and Catholic, with lots of Caribbean mixed in. Founded by a French explorer in 1718, French colonists followed and established the port. They left their mark, including a fondness for butter and cream and a legacy of provincial French recipes adapted to local ingredients. Later, the Spanish ruled New Orleans for decades, layering their culinary traditions onto those of its French inhabitants. Then the Acadians arrived from Nova Scotia in the mid-1800s and settled in south Louisiana's bayous. With their own French heritage, they developed a unique cooking style based on living off the land and using whatever ingredients they grew, caught or trapped.

Add to this tropical foods and fiery seasonings from the West Indies and Africa introduced by black cooks in the kitchens of slave owners. By the time New Orleans joined the United States, courtesy of the Louisiana Purchase in 1803, these culinary influences had all combined in an exciting, ethnic-based cooking tradition.

Generally speaking, New Orleans cooking divides into two styles, Creole and Cajun, but I'll warn you that the line between them often blurs. It just depends who's in the kitchen and where he or she learned to cook. Creole cooking is city cooking. It's the style that evolved from classic continental French cooking paired with native ingredients and herbs. Some folks think it's more refined due to the aristocratic influences of early French and Spanish settlers. Over the years, cooking traditions from Spain, Africa, Germany, Italy and England have made Creole cooking the hybrid style evident in its gumbos and jambalayas.

Cajun cooking, however, although also French-inspired, is country cooking. It's rural, home-style, wet, spicy, strong, peppery and equally delicious. Cajun cooking may use one pot for practically the whole meal and its ingredients come straight from farms, gardens and waterways. That's why you'll find crawfish, catfish, crab, shrimp and oysters, ducks, frogs, homemade sausages, beans and rice as staples in this earthy cuisine.

As much as they are distinctive and as much as they overlap, the secret to both Creole and Cajun cooking is in their seasonings. They play a subtle or starring role in the dishes I've included here, from a Filé Gumbo to Shrimp Jambalaya and Crawfish Cardinal. So indulge your senses by tasting a bit of New Orleans' fire and flavor. I know you'll savor every bite.

Beignets

MAKES **20** BEIGNETS

THE REST OF THE COUNTRY MAY HAVE doughnuts, sopaipillas, or fritters, but New Orleans has its beignets and oh, how tasty they are! You'll find them by the dozens at restaurants all around the French Market and Jackson Square. Enjoy these airy, deep-fried pastries by dipping them into a bowl of powdered sugar and then wash them down with a cup of dark French-roast coffee, New Orleans-style. Older recipes call for evaporated milk to enrich the taste, but knowing Louisiana's heat, the canned milk was probably a godsend in the days before everyone had refrigerators. Either way, you'll love this New Orleans classic.

1   quart corn oil

2   cups flour

1   teaspoon salt

1   tablespoon baking powder

1   teaspoon ground cinnamon

1   medium egg

3   tablespoons sugar

1   cup milk

¼   teaspoon vanilla extract

Confectioner's sugar for dusting

Half fill a large, deep pot with the corn oil and bring to 375°F over medium heat.

Sift together the flour, salt, baking powder and cinnamon into a large mixing bowl. In a small mixing bowl, beat the egg. Add the sugar, milk and vanilla extract. Pour the egg mixture into the flour mixture and stir to combine. Turn the dough onto a floured surface and knead lightly. Roll the dough out to ¼-inch thickness and slice into diamond shapes about 3 inches long.

Fry the beignets, a few at a time, in the oil, turning once, for 4 to 6 minutes, until golden brown. Remove with a slotted spoon and drain on paper towels. Dust with the confectioner's sugar and serve immediately.

Boudin Balls

SERVES 6 TO 8

LOUSIANA'S SAVORY WHITE-MEAT sausage, boudin, has origins in France where it is a Christmas specialty. While the French filling is a combination of poultry, veal, pork or rabbit meat, thrifty Cajuns adapted the ingredients to use just pork and added cayenne pepper to satisfy their love of hot-hot-hot! Since sausage-making is something that requires a fair amount of perseverance and special equipment, I suggest forming the meat into balls and frying them to enjoy the zesty flavor with less effort.

½ cup chopped onion

½ cup finely chopped green onions

½ cup finely chopped fresh parsley

1 tablespoon finely chopped garlic

3 tablespoons olive or peanut oil

1½ cups water

3 cups cooked white rice

5 cups finely chopped cooked pork

½ teaspoon salt

⅛ teaspoon cayenne pepper

4 egg whites

1 quart corn oil

In a large, heavy pot placed over medium heat, sauté the onion, green onions, parsley and garlic in the olive oil for 5 minutes. Stir in the water, rice, pork, salt and cayenne. Bring to a simmer, cover and cook for 10 minutes.

Turn the pork mixture into a large bowl. When it is cool enough to handle, using your hands, mix in the egg whites. Form 2-inch balls and place on a baking sheet. When all the balls are formed, refrigerate for 1 hour.

Bring the corn oil to 350°F in a deep pot placed over medium heat. Drop the balls in the hot oil, about 5 at a time, for 3 to 5 minutes, until they begin to brown. Remove with a slotted spoon, drain briefly on paper towels and serve.

Spicy Fried Shrimp Remoulade

SERVES 4

WITH THE GULF OF MEXICO BEING *a perfect happy home for shrimp, Louisiana's fishermen catch half of the nation's annual harvest. Sweet and succulent, shrimp in a variety of forms are standard fare on most New Orleans' menus. The deep-fried, butterflied version here, with its crunchy cornmeal coating, is particularly delicious with a classic remoulade sauce. This is a creamy, mayonnaise-like dressing always made with mustard. Like many continental French dishes, Louisianans have made it their own by adding hot and tingly seasonings.*

SAUCE
- 3 tablespoons ketchup
- 3 tablespoons mayonnaise
- 3 tablespoons coarse mustard
- 2 tablespoons white vinegar
- 2 tablespoons horseradish
- 1 tablespoon Worcestershire sauce
- 1 teaspoon hot pepper sauce (such as Tabasco)
- 2 tablespoons minced green onions
- 2 tablespoons minced celery
- 2 tablespoons minced fresh parsley

SHRIMP
- 2 cups flour
- 1 tablespoon cayenne pepper
- 2 eggs
- 1 cup milk
- 1 cup cornmeal
- 1 quart corn oil
- 1 pound large shrimp, peeled, tail on, deveined

FOR SAUCE: In a small mixing bowl, combine all of the ingredients for the sauce. Cover and refrigerate until ready to serve.

FOR SHRIMP: Combine 1 cup of the flour and the cayenne pepper in a wide, shallow bowl. In another bowl, beat the eggs with the milk. In a third bowl, mix the remaining cup of flour and the cornmeal. Place the oil in a deep pot over medium heat and bring to 375°F. Rinse and dry the shrimp. Roll the shrimp in the flour mixture, being sure to cover the insides of the cut portion. Dip into the egg wash and then dredge in the cornmeal and flour. Open each shrimp at the cut and lightly press down to help the mixture stick.

Fry the shrimp, 5 or 6 at a time, in the oil for 3 to 5 minutes, until golden brown. Remove with a slotted spoon and drain on paper towels. Serve immediately alongside a bowl filled with the remoulade sauce.

Crab and Crawfish Cardinal

SERVES 6

ONCE UPON A TIME IN LOUISIANA, crawfish were looked down on as "poor man's shrimp." But one enterprising New Orleans businessman put them on a restaurant menu in 1935 and practically overnight, crawfish became a "must eat" sensation. Think of this crustacean as almost the freshwater equivalent of lobster. Crawfish do not travel well and about 95 percent are produced and eaten in Louisiana. Shrimp is an acceptable substitute. If you do find crawfish, be prepared to shell a lot for the amount of meat you need. Prepared here "wetlands-style" with a classic roux and served with rice, another Louisiana staple, this delicious dish is well worth the effort.

8 tablespoons unsalted butter

4 tablespoons flour

1 cup milk

½ cup heavy cream

½ teaspoon salt

⅛ teaspoon white pepper

2 green onions, finely chopped

¼ cup white wine

¼ cup tomato sauce

½ pound lump crabmeat, drained, picked over

1 pound cleaned cooked crawfish (crayfish) tails (if available) or cooked medium shrimp

¼ teaspoon salt

⅛ teaspoon cayenne pepper

6 cups hot cooked rice

In a small, heavy saucepot placed over medium heat, melt 4 tablespoons of the butter. Add the flour and stir to make a paste. Cook the roux for 1 minute, or until it starts to turn light brown. Turn off the heat and then whisk in the milk. When the mixture is blended, return the pot to low heat and let simmer for 5 minutes. Add the cream, the ½ teaspoon of salt and the white pepper. Let the sauce simmer for 2 more minutes.

In a large, heavy skillet, sauté the green onions in the remaining 4 tablespoons of butter for 1 minute over medium-high heat. Add the white wine and tomato sauce, turn the heat to medium-low and cook for 5 minutes. Stir in the cream sauce, raise the heat to medium and bring to a simmer. Add the crabmeat, crawfish, salt and cayenne. Cook for 2 to 3 minutes, until the shellfish are heated through.

Serve immediately over hot cooked rice.

Filé Gumbo

THE NAME OF THIS HEARTY STEW, "gumbo," comes from the African Bantu word for okra, a pod-like vegetable used for its thickening effect. In Louisiana, gumbo is made with either okra or filé powder; never both. Land and sea unite in gumbo's ingredients, which traditionally included anything in the kitchen according to the whim of the cook. The Creole version of this one-pot dish starts with a light-colored roux and uses "filé," or powdered sassafras, for seasoning. A tip about filé is not to let it cook for long, or the broth will turn gummy. Add it only just before you are ready to serve.

8	tablespoons unsalted butter
½	cup chopped celery
½	cup chopped onion
¼	cup flour
8	cups fish stock
¼	pound smoked ham, diced
¼	pound Creole hot sausage, sliced
¼	pound andouille sausage, sliced
½	pound large shrimp, peeled, cleaned
½	pound lump crabmeat, drained, picked over
½	teaspoon salt
½	teaspoon freshly ground pepper
1	tablespoon minced fresh parsley
1	tablespoon filé powder
4	cups hot cooked rice

Melt the butter in a deep, heavy pot placed over medium-low heat. Add the celery and onion and sauté for 3 minutes. Stir in the flour and cook for 5 minutes. Remove the pot from the heat and slowly whisk in the fish stock. Return the pot to the heat and bring to a simmer. Simmer for 20 minutes, stirring occasionally. Add the ham and sausages and continue to cook for another 20 minutes.

Gently stir in the shrimp, crabmeat, salt, pepper, parsley and filé powder. Return the gumbo to a low simmer for 2 minutes. Ladle the gumbo over ½ cup of the hot rice for each portion and serve immediately.

Shrimp Jambalaya

SERVES 4

THE VARIATIONS OF THIS DISH ARE as numerous as gumbo and its history just as colorful. "Jamba" is taken from the French "jambon" and Spanish "jamon," both words for ham. Add "à la," meaning "in the manner of" in French, and "ya," an African word for rice and an expletive, and there's the word. A simple translation might be "ham with rice, yeah-yeah." When it comes right down to it, jambalaya is basically a Louisiana interpretation of Spanish paella that uses local ingredients, the three essentials tradition- ally being chicken, rice and tomatoes. After that anything goes. In my version, I've used shrimp, but feel free to add any other meat, fish, sausage or poultry you desire.

1	cup finely chopped onions
¼	cup finely chopped green onions
2	tablespoons finely chopped green bell pepper
2	teaspoons finely chopped garlic
¼	cup corn oil
1	8-ounce can tomato sauce
1	cup raw white rice
2	cups shrimp stock or water
2	teaspoons Worcestershire sauce
	Salt to taste
	Hot pepper sauce (such as Tabasco) to taste
1	pound shrimp, peeled, deveined
¼	cup finely chopped fresh parsley

In a medium-size, heavy pot placed over medium heat, sauté the onions, green onions, bell pepper and garlic in the oil. When the onions are clear, after about 5 minutes, stir in the tomato sauce. Bring to a simmer and add the rice, stock, Worcestershire sauce, salt and hot sauce. When it returns to a simmer, cover, reduce the heat to low and cook for 10 minutes.

After most of the liquid has been absorbed, gently stir in the shrimp and parsley, cover and cook for another 5 minutes. When all of the liquid has been absorbed, remove from the heat and let the jambalaya steam for another 5 minutes, then serve.

Red Beans and Rice

THIS IS ANOTHER CLASSIC New Orleans dish with an interesting past. I'm told it was tradition-ally eaten for Monday supper—to soak up the hangover lingering from too much partying Saturday night, to use up the Sunday dinner ham bone, and to spare the cook from standing over a hot stove after a day spent doing the laundry. Rice displaced corn and wheat in Louisiana diets since it grew so easily in the state's swampy wetlands, and beans were readily available and filling. Although this combination is considered "po-man's" food, it's one of those satisfying simple dishes that's been re-discovered and gone "upscale" today.

1   cup dried kidney beans

1   quart water

1   cup chopped onions

½   cup chopped green bell pepper

½   cup chopped green onions

1   bay leaf

½   teaspoon thyme

2   garlic cloves, minced

¼   teaspoon freshly ground pepper

6   ounces ham, cut into ½-inch cubes

2   cups hot cooked rice

Soak the beans in the water overnight in a large pot. The next day, add all the remaining ingredients except the rice and place over medium heat. Bring to a simmer, cover and cook for 1½ hours. Add more water if the mixture becomes dry.

To serve, place about ½ cup of the rice on each plate and ladle the red beans with ham in the center.

Butter Beans

SERVES 4 TO 6

PERHAPS IF LIMA BEANS HAD BEEN *named "butter beans" from the start, a lot of children would have grown up liking them better. Certainly they'd love this slightly sweet vegetable dish that might be considered the Cajun version of Boston baked beans. Be sure to use blackstrap molasses. Although it has the least amount of sugar of all molasses varieties, blackstrap molasses produced from sugar cane grown in Louisiana has the most distinctive and richest taste. Used with beans and diced vegetables, it adds flavor to a simple side dish that complements chicken, pork or seafood.*

8 tablespoons butter

2 strips bacon, chopped

2 cups chopped onions

1 tablespoon minced garlic

¼ cup finely diced carrots

¼ cup finely diced celery

½ teaspoon cayenne pepper

½ teaspoon freshly ground pepper

3½ cups fresh lima beans

6 cups chicken broth

1 teaspoon blackstrap molasses

Melt the butter in a large, deep pot placed over medium heat. Add the bacon and sauté for 5 minutes. Stir in the onions, garlic, carrots, celery, cayenne and pepper and cook for 10 minutes.

Add the beans and 1 cup of the chicken broth. Cover and simmer for 10 minutes. Remove the cover and simmer until almost all of the liquid has evaporated. Stir well, turn the heat to high and add the remaining chicken broth and the molasses. Bring the mixture to a boil and cook, stirring often, for 30 minutes, until the beans are tender.

Raisin Cake with Rum Sauce

SERVES 6 TO 8

NEW ORLEANS' DESSERT LEGACY probably stems more from its citified Creole traditions than from the bayou country's robust Cajun cooking. Certainly by the 1890s, the city's cooks were competing to see who could bake the most splendid cake for the dessert course at a "small Creole dinner" that might include ten or more courses. The tradition is carried on in this rich vanilla loaf cake that resembles a pound cake. Since the flavors of the Caribbean are very much a part of New Orleans cooking, a sauce made with rum from the islands adds a sophisticated accent.

CAKE

- 1 cup unsalted butter, room temperature
- 1 cup sugar
- 2 teaspoons vanilla extract
- 1 cup self-rising flour
- ½ cup all-purpose flour
- ½ cup raisins
- 3 eggs

SAUCE

- ½ cup unsalted butter
- 2 tablespoons flour
- ¼ cup sugar
- ⅓ cup dark rum

FOR CAKE: Preheat the oven to 325°F. Coat a 9 x 4 x 3-inch loaf pan with butter and place a piece of waxed paper on the bottom.

Cream the butter and sugar in the bowl of an electric mixer until it is smooth, about 5 minutes. Add the vanilla extract.

In a small mixing bowl, combine the flours and raisins. Add the eggs one at a time to the butter mixture, alternating with the flour mixture, until it is all blended in.

Pour the batter into the prepared baking pan and place in the oven for 1 hour. Remove to a metal rack and let the cake cool before removing it from the pan.

FOR SAUCE: While the cake is baking, prepare the sauce. Melt the butter in a small pot over low heat. Add the flour, stir well and cook for 3 minutes. Whisk in the sugar and rum and bring to a boil, whisking constantly. Remove from the heat.

When the cake has cooled but is still slightly warm, cut into 1-inch-thick slices, drizzle with some rum sauce and serve.

Praline Sundae

SERVES 6 TO 8

PRALINES ARE TO NEW ORLEANS what saltwater taffy is to the New England seashore: a classic candy that no one can resist. Traditionally sold on street corners around Jackson Square by pralinières, *they have always been a favorite children's sweet. Pralines can be made with either white sugar and freshly grated coconut, or creamy caramelized brown sugar and crunchy pecans. The same ingredients are also sometimes used to make a sauce or dessert garnish. I've adapted the melt-in-your-mouth buttery sweetness of brown sugar pecan pralines here into an irresistible sundae.*

1 cup sugar

1 cup dark corn syrup

1 cup unsalted butter

2 teaspoons vanilla extract

2 cups pecan halves

1 pint vanilla ice cream

In a medium-size, heavy pot over medium heat, bring the sugar, corn syrup and butter to a boil. Lower the heat and simmer for 3 to 5 minutes, until the sugar is dissolved. Remove from the heat and stir in the vanilla extract and pecans.

Place a generous scoop of the ice cream in a dish, cover with the praline sauce and serve immediately.

KANSAS CITY

Kansas City Steak Soup

Smokey Beans

Molasses-Mustard Chicken

Backwagon Sauce

Rubbed Baby Back Ribs

Big Sky Sauce for Game

Kansas City Strip Steak

Dirt Pie

Horseradish and Green Bean Salad

Smack in the middle of the country is where you'll find Kansas City, sitting proudly in the center of America's heartland. It's a great town sprawling over the riverbanks at the junction of the Kansas and Missouri rivers on the edge of acres and acres of fertile farmlands and wheat fields rolling their way west. The rivers, along with Kansas City, were vital to opening the western half of the United States, an emigration process that changed forever the size, shape and destiny of this country.

From 1830 to 1840, Kansas City was a jumping off point for the great wagon train trails westward: the Oregon Trail, the Santa Fe Trail and the California Trail. Over 150,000 settlers traveled to the western frontier in wagon trains departing from Kansas City, doubling the country's geographical size. Despite stories and legends to the contrary, more than 90 percent of them made the journey safely.

The city actually got its start in 1833 as Westport, the site of a trading post and boat dock and now a historic district in town. French fur traders, mountain men from the Ozarks, Native Americans, farmers, and boatmen from St. Louis and Independence all stopped enroute to stock up on supplies for their westward or northern journeys. In 1853, the state of Missouri officially incorporated the area as the City of Kansas. During the Civil War, because Kansas Territory, lying one mile to the west, was free and Missouri was a slave state, many free or escaped slaves also migrated to the area. It was a rough and tumble river town, a melting pot even back then and that diversity has certainly contributed to its culinary traditions.

As farming boomed in Kansas, Iowa, and Nebraska, and vast ranches to the West shipped their cattle to eastern cities, Kansas City became a railroad hub and a center for cattle and wholesale grain markets accompanied by livestock show barns, stockyards and meat-packing plants. Being the center of America's agricultural world, meat and all its various preparations—from T-bone to strip steak, chops and roast, to shoulder, brisket and ribs—are at the heart of Kansas City's culinary traditions. Keeping working men well fed is a significant business and the city has always had great steak houses and restaurants.

But what really distinguishes this town is its barbecue. Now I know barbecue is a touchy subject and there can be endless debates, even wars, about what makes one style better than another. But in this part of the country, the tradition runs deep.

Along with barbecue you'll find smoked meats showing up in other dishes like the local version of baked beans. Even cooking chicken is influenced by Kansas City's barbecue traditions when it's marinated with a sweet-savory sauce and then grilled. Everyone, it seems, has his or her own "rub," or marinade sauce and doesn't mind sharing, so I've included a few typical sauces in the selection of recipes here. You'll also note some ethnic influences from Kansas City's era as an immigrant melting pot in the use of horseradish and ancho chilies. After trying these recipes, I think you'll agree that Kansas City has a great all-American culinary tradition and I'm pleased to pass it on.

Kansas City Steak Soup

SERVES 8 TO 10

IN ITS BUSTLING COW TOWN ERA, Kansas City built a legacy as a town where steak was king. Hand-cut and aged prime beef steaks were on the menu at every restaurant, and many prepared their own steaks right on the premises. Cattlemen and businessmen alike enjoyed the tender cuts of beef, sometimes at two meals a day. But with all the steaks being prepared, there needed to be some way to use up the steak trimmings. A practical cook created what is basically a spicy vegetable soup with the steak trimmings cooked until tender. Southwestern culinary influences show up in the use of spicy chili beans and cumin.

1 pound London broil, cut into ½-inch cubes

1 onion, chopped

1 garlic clove, minced

2 tablespoons corn oil

1 teaspoon ground cumin

1 14½-ounce can crushed tomatoes

1 15-ounce can spicy chili beans

8 ounces beef broth

½ cup sour cream

In a deep, heavy pot placed over medium-high heat, sauté the beef, onion and garlic in the corn oil until the meat is brown on all sides, about 5 to 7 minutes. Stir in the cumin and cook for another 2 minutes. Add the tomatoes, chili beans and broth. Bring to a boil. Lower the heat until it just simmers and cook for 15 minutes. Adjust the thickness with a little more beef broth or water.

Serve with a dollop of sour cream in the center of each bowl of soup.

Molasses-Mustard Chicken

SERVES 4

Kansas sits in the heartland of America, a crossroads of pioneer wagon trails, railroads, highways, and of course, culinary influences. This recipe, with a marinade using mustard, vinegar and blackstrap molasses, shows its southern origins. Molasses was used as an affordable sweetener before white sugar was widely available. Blackstrap molasses is thick, rich and more intense than regular molasses since it's taken at the end of the sugar cane refining process. Even a small amount adds a wonderful taste. Grilled on a barbecue, this chicken dish is downright mouthwatering.

3 tablespoons blackstrap molasses

3 tablespoons Dijon-style mustard

1 tablespoon cider vinegar

1 tablespoon chopped fresh thyme or
   1 teaspoon dried

2 skinless boneless chicken
   breasts, halved

1 teaspoon salt

½ teaspoon freshly ground pepper

In a small bowl, combine the molasses, mustard, vinegar and thyme. Pound the chicken to an even ½-inch thickness. Sprinkle with the salt and pepper. In a large, shallow dish, coat the chicken with the molasses mixture. Cover and refrigerate for 2 hours.

Bring the grill to medium-high heat. Brush a little oil on the grill rack and cook the chicken, 4 to 6 minutes on each side, basting as it cooks.

Serve straight from the grill.

Rubbed Baby Back Ribs

SERVES 6

KANSAS CITY'S BARBECUE TRADITION dates to the 1930s when city culinary legends like Henry Potter custom slow-smoked ribs and brisket for customers. One of Kansas City's claims to fame today is baby back pork ribs that have been coated with a spice rub and then slow-smoked for hours until tender. Every cook has his or her own favorite "rub" mixture and some are quite secretive about the ingredients. One essential trick to ensure great taste: take a pair of needlenose pliers and pull off the membrane from the back of a chilled rib rack so that the smoke from the grill can permeate the meat better and make it more tender.

2 cups sugar

¼ cup paprika

½ teaspoon chili powder

1 teaspoon lemon pepper

½ teaspoon cayenne pepper

¼ cup salt

1 teaspoon garlic powder

4 slabs (about 6 pounds) baby back ribs

In a small mixing bowl, combine all of the ingredients except the ribs. Coat the ribs generously with the rub and place them in 2 shallow roasting pans.

Preheat the oven to 350°F. Bake the ribs for 1½ hours. Remove from the oven and drain off the fat. Add another coat of the rub. Bring the barbecue to a medium-high heat and grill the ribs 4 inches from the heat. Cook for 10 minutes, then turn over and cook for another 10 minutes.

Cut into 2-rib serving portions.

Kansas City Strip Steak

SERVES 2 TO 3

BEFORE THE 20TH CENTURY, *beef was a luxury for all but a few, esteemed because of its English heritage and implications of wealth. As Americans pushed west to the prairies, the wide open spaces gave rise to vast wheat fields plus great cattle ranches that produced beef in huge quantities to satisfy big city markets in the East. As a crossroads for this enterprise, Kansas City has a colorful cow town past and a legacy of great steaks. Several of the city's steak restaurants, like the Golden Ox near the old stockyards and Hereford House, downtown, served local Kansas City strip steaks, hand-cut and aged on their premises. This preparation includes a traditional marinade.*

2 12-ounce strip steaks
1 tablespoon freshly ground pepper
1 tablespoon Worcestershire sauce
1 tablespoon beef broth
¼ cup water
2 tablespoons red wine vinegar
1 tablespoon brown sugar
⅓ cup ketchup
¼ teaspoon cayenne pepper

Pat dry the steaks and coat both sides with the pepper. Place in a shallow roasting pan. In a small bowl, combine the Worcestershire sauce, beef broth, water and red wine vinegar. Pour over the steaks, cover and refrigerate for 20 minutes. Turn the steaks after 10 minutes.

In a small bowl, whisk together the brown sugar, ketchup and cayenne pepper.

Bring the grill to medium heat. Remove the steaks from the marinade and brush one side with the barbecue sauce. Place the steaks, sauce side down, 4 inches from the heat for 5 minutes for rare, 8 for medium. Baste the top side with the remaining sauce. Turn and cook for another 5 or 8 minutes.

Allow the steaks to rest for 5 minutes if you are going to cut them to serve more than 2 people. Otherwise, serve immediately.

Horseradish and Green Bean Salad

SERVES 4 TO 6

POPULAR THROUGHOUT MUCH of Europe, Eastern Europe and Russia, horseradish came to the United States along with immigrants from these parts of the world, so it's no surprise to find it in Kansas City kitchens. Used here in its prepared form as a seasoning, grated horseradish adds a lively taste to a simple preparation of market fresh green beans. Of course, it's even better if you have green beans to use from your garden, but either way I recommend the result as a delicious side dish to serve with steak or chicken.

1   pound fresh green beans, trimmed

3   tablespoons butter, melted

1   tablespoon cider vinegar

2   tablespoons prepared horseradish

Bring a large pot of water to a boil over high heat. Add the green beans and cook for 5 to 7 minutes. While the beans are cooking, combine the butter, vinegar and horseradish in a small bowl. Drain the beans and rinse with cold water.

In a medium-size bowl, toss the beans with the horseradish mixture. Cover and refrigerate until ready to serve.

The beans can also be served hot. Simply omit the cold rinse after cooking and immediately toss with the horseradish and serve.

Smokey Beans

JUST AS KANSANS ARE PARTIAL to slow-smoked ribs and brisket, they're also fond of beans that are smoked rather than baked New England-style. They start with a classic baked bean recipe, but, as you might expect, add bits of chopped barbecued meats instead of bacon or pork. Instead of ketchup or tomato sauce, barbecue sauce is the preferred flavoring ingredient. Slow-cooked for hours, the result is a savory treat served with steak or barbecued ribs. I've adapted a traditional recipe here for an easy-to-prepare version for contemporary cooks. The result is equally tasty!

4 strips bacon, chopped

½ cup diced onions

2 tablespoons dry mustard

2 16-ounce cans baked beans

1 tablespoon Worcestershire sauce

½ teaspoon liquid smoke

½ cup diced green bell pepper

In a heavy skillet over medium heat, cook the bacon and onions for 5 to 7 minutes, until the onions are soft and translucent. Stir in the dry mustard and cook for 2 minutes. Add the baked beans, Worcestershire sauce and liquid smoke. Bring to a boil, lower the heat and simmer for 10 minutes. Remove from the heat, stir in the green pepper and serve.

Backwagon Sauce

1 tablespoon corn oil

½ medium onion, chopped

½ celery rib, chopped

1 garlic clove, minced

1 tablespoon chili powder

1 tablespoon brown sugar

1 teaspoon dried oregano

½ cup beef broth

¼ cup ketchup

¼ cup chili sauce

2 tablespoons cider vinegar

¼ teaspoon hot pepper sauce

Place all of the ingredients in a blender or food processor and puree until smooth.

Brush the sauce on meats during the last 20 minutes of grilling.

Big Sky Sauce for Game

MAKES 1⅔ CUPS

1½ dried ancho chilies

1 cup beef broth

1 tablespoon chopped oil-packed sun-dried tomatoes

3 garlic cloves

½ small onion, chopped

2 teaspoons dried oregano

2 teaspoons dark brown sugar

2 tablespoons tomato paste

1 tablespoon red wine vinegar

In a small bowl, soak the chilies in the beef broth for 15 minutes. When they are soft, place all of the ingredients in a food processor or blender and puree until smooth.

Brush the sauce on game and meats during the last 20 minutes of grilling.

Dirt Pie

I HAD TO CHECK TWICE WHEN I heard about this dessert, but it really exists and is a favorite from Kansas to Colorado with many delicious variations ranging from cake to pie with ice cream or whipped cream — and it's not served just to kids! Adults love it, too. Depending on the ingredients, it's traditionally made and served in one big clay flower pot or several small flower pots (all clean, of course) for individual servings, or even a child's beach bucket. Some people top the concoction in its flower pot form with a real flower, while others hide Gummi worm candies in the "soil" section. To give the dessert a bit more sophistication, I've prepared it in a graham cracker pie crust.

1 cup cold milk

1 4-ounce package instant chocolate pudding

8 ounces whipped topping (such as Cool Whip)

20 chocolate sandwich cookies, crushed

1½ cups mixture of granola, chocolate chips and peanut butter chips

1 9-inch prepared graham cracker pie crust

Whisk together the milk and chocolate pudding mix in a medium-size bowl. Let stand for 5 minutes. Fold in the whipped topping, 1 cup of the crushed sandwich cookies and the granola mixture. Pour into the prepared pie crust. Sprinkle with the remaining sandwich cookie crumbs and freeze for 4 hours, until firm.

To serve, place a large knife under hot running water and slice.

SEATTLE

Sweet and Sour Coconut Prawns

Dungeness Crab with
Lemon Ginger Sauce

Broiled Halibut with
Spicy Sake Sauce

Ginger Poached Salmon

Chicken Satay

Fennel Sautéed with Onions
and Bacon

Confettied Chard

Spiced Apple Bread Pudding

I visited Seattle's famous Pike Place Public Market in early summer on my first trip to the Northwest. It's one of the oldest public farmers' markets in the country, a cultural legacy, where foods from farms and fields and ocean intersect and the bounty of the Northwest arrives fresh everyday.

But I wasn't prepared for the hustle and bustle, the colorful stalls and tables overflowing with top quality seafood, lush produce, beautiful flowers, and the craftspeople with all their wares. It's a truly remarkable place where you find shoppers and, of course, tourists like me, meeting face to face with hardworking farmers, many now from Vietnam and China, and entertaining fishmongers. You can taste, smell, dream and then buy everything you need to take home and make a fabulous dinner.

Strolling the Market, I sampled new peas, cherries from the state's eastern orchards, local honeys, dark red Northwestern strawberries. I saw Asian immigrant farmers offering a host of greens and exotic vegetables like lotus root and Japanese eggplant used in their homelands. Then there are the five species of sleek silver salmon (true Seattle-ites can name them all). Piled on ice or sailing through the air as the fish guys literally toss and catch a customer's selection at the counter, these amazing fish are beautiful to behold. Plus, feisty plump Dungeness crab, enormous king crab legs, shrimp, sea bass, black cod, rock fish and halibut are all delivered fresh from icy Alaskan waters.

Native Americans were first to discover the Northwest's natural bounty of foodstuffs. They ate what they could catch from the sea or harvest from the forests. Waves of European immigrants arrived in the mid to late 1800s and many were farmers. They found a region blessed by, fertile volcanic soil in eastern farmlands, a long, temperate growing season, and the famous Northwest rain. Gentle showers and snow in the Cascade mountains all winter long provide water to irrigate the state's dry eastern and southern valleys where apples, pears, cherries, grapes, wheat, asparagus and a variety of other vegetables grow.

Blessed with all these high-quality ingredients, Northwesterners follow the rule of "simple is better" when preparing food. Maybe it's the influence of the straightforward Scandinavians who arrived in the 1880s, but most cooks in this sophisticated city think there's little need to overwhelm regional foods by adding more flavors.

However, with all the immigrants arriving in the past 25 years from Southeast Asia, you quickly discover that Asian flavors have also become popular. Some local chefs have led the way, showing how deliciously flavors from Thailand, Japan and China pair with regional foods. Some even say Pacific Rim and fusion cuisine first started here, before California. I think it was probably a tie, but Asian flavors are becoming a natural part of northwestern cooking.

But now you can get a taste of it yourself with the recipes that follow. I bet you'll be making these dishes more than once. They're that good!

Sweet and Sour Coconut Prawns

SERVES 4 TO 6

THIS SCRUMPTIOUS APPETIZER SHOWS the culinary influence recent Southeast Asian immigrants have had on Pacific Northwest cuisine by introducing the sweet-savory concept with ginger, garlic and brown sugar. Mild, sweet Spot prawns from the cold waters of Puget Sound or southeast Alaska are preferred if they're available, but any large shrimp will do.

1 cup pineapple juice

¼ cup rice wine vinegar

¼ cup soy sauce

⅓ cup dark brown sugar

2 teaspoons freshly grated gingerroot

2 garlic cloves, minced

2 tablespoons cornstarch

1½ pounds large shrimp (about 18 to 20)

1 cup flour

½ teaspoon cayenne pepper

4 eggs, beaten

2 cups shredded coconut

3 cups corn oil

2 cups peanut oil

In a small pot placed over medium heat, whisk together the pineapple juice, vinegar, soy sauce, brown sugar, ginger, garlic and cornstarch. Whisking constantly, bring to a boil for 2 minutes. Remove from the heat but keep warm until ready to serve.

Peel the shrimp, leaving the tails on. With a sharp, small knife, cut halfway through along the backs of the shrimp. Rinse out the veins under running cold water. Pat dry with paper towels.

Using wide shallow bowls, combine the flour and cayenne pepper in one, the beaten eggs in another and the coconut in the last.

Dredge the butterflied shrimp in the flour, dip in the egg wash, and roll in the coconut. Place each prepared shrimp on a large plate. At this point, the shrimp can be covered with plastic wrap and refrigerated until time to fry.

Bring the oils to 375°F in a deep, heavy pot. Place 5 to 6 shrimp in the oil. Cook for 3 to 5 minutes, until golden. Remove with a slotted spoon and drain on paper towels while you cook the remaining shrimp.

Place the shrimp on individual serving plates and set a small bowl with some of the sweet and sour sauce on each. Serve while still warm.

Dungeness Crab with Lemon Ginger Sauce

SERVES 4

FORGET THE TABLECLOTH AND NAPKINS to eat this Northwest favorite. I learned to simply cover a table with newspaper, tie on a paper bib and start cracking the bright orange shells and licking my fingers the way the natives do. Boiling is the traditional preparation method for these crabs found from northern California to Alaska. Crab season varies all along the coast, so you'll find succulent Dungeness crabs available in the markets almost year-round. If you're buying crabs live from a fish tank, look for plump, heavy ones that are active.

4 2-pound Dungeness crabs

3 tablespoons fresh lemon juice

Zest of 1 lemon

Pinch salt

1 teaspoon Dijon-style mustard

1 tablespoon rice wine vinegar

1 tablespoon freshly grated gingerroot

2 teaspoons honey

3 tablespoons olive oil

3 tablespoons peanut oil

Bring a large pot filled with salted water to a boil over high heat. Submerge the crabs and cook for 5 minutes. Lift out of the water. When they are cool enough to handle, begin taking them apart. Break off the top shell. Rinse and remove the gills. Break the body in half. Remove the tail apron from the bottom shell.

Place the lemon juice, zest, salt, mustard, rice wine vinegar, ginger and honey in the bowl of a food processor. Pulse until smooth. With the motor running, slowly add the oils to form a vinaigrette sauce.

Serve the crabs with a small bowl of lemon ginger sauce on each plate.

Broiled Halibut with Spicy Sake Sauce

SERVES 4

WHEN THE FIRST HALIBUT ARRIVES FROM ALASKA in early spring, eager Seattle-ites line up at fish counters in the Pike Place market or their local grocery store to buy steaks and fillets of this popular white fish. Although available frozen year-round, fresh halibut has a dense, meaty texture and rich, subtle flavor that is unmistakable and remarkably delicious. These characteristics make halibut prized for its ability to adapt beautifully to the spicy Pacific Rim flavors of soy and sake. When making this dish, be sure not to overcook the fish.

2 garlic cloves, minced

1 tablespoon minced green onions (white part only)

2 tablespoons peanut oil

½ cup sake

2 tablespoons soy sauce

2 tablespoons rice wine vinegar

¼ cup chicken broth

2 teaspoons cornstarch

2 pounds halibut fillets, cut into 4 pieces

1 teaspoon freshly ground pepper

2 green onions (green part only), cut into thin long strips for garnish

In a heavy skillet set over medium heat, sauté the garlic and minced green onions in 1 tablespoon of the peanut oil for 2 minutes. Add the sake and simmer for 1 minute. Combine the soy sauce, rice wine vinegar, chicken broth and cornstarch in a small bowl. Stir to dissolve the cornstarch. Slowly add the mixture to the skillet. Stir the sauce and bring to a simmer for 2 minutes. Remove from the heat but keep warm.

Preheat the broiler. Brush both sides of the halibut fillets with the remaining peanut oil, sprinkle with the pepper and place on a broiling pan or a metal rack set in a shallow roasting pan. Place the fish 3 inches from the broiler and cook for 4 to 5 minutes on each side, until the fish is firm but not dry.

Serve each fillet with a couple of tablespoons of the sauce on top. Garnish with a few strips of the green onions.

Ginger Poached Salmon

SERVES 6

SILVER-SIDED SALMON ARE A NORTHWEST ICON. Wild salmon jumping above waterfalls and battling rapids to swim upstream are awesome in the fierce migration that takes them from fresh water stream to the ocean for two to three years, then home again to spawn so the cycle can be repeated by the next generation. These salmon are prized for their rich flavor and buttery texture that pairs well with Pan-Pacific flavors.

1 quart water

½ lemon, thinly sliced

½ cup mirin (sweet rice wine)

1 3-inch piece gingerroot, peeled, thinly sliced

2 green onions, chopped

½ cup sesame seeds

2 teaspoons finely grated gingerroot

1 tablespoon sesame oil

2 teaspoons cornstarch

1 tablespoon lemon juice

1 tablespoon soy sauce

2 cups chicken or fish broth

⅓ cup sliced green onions

6 ½-pound, skinless pieces salmon fillets

Bring the water, sliced lemon, mirin, sliced ginger and chopped green onions to a boil in a large, shallow pan over high heat. Cover and boil for 5 minutes. Turn off the heat and let steep for 10 minutes.

Toast the sesame seeds over low heat in a wide skillet. Shake frequently and remove from the pan as soon as they begin to turn brown, about 3 to 5 minutes.

To prepare the sauce, puree ¼ cup of the sesame seeds, the grated ginger and sesame oil in a food processor. In a small pot over medium heat, whisking constantly, bring the cornstarch, lemon juice, soy sauce and broth to a boil. Lower the heat and simmer for 5 minutes. Add the sesame seed paste and sliced green onions, simmer for 3 more minutes and then remove the sauce from the heat.

Bring the poaching liquid to a boil and add 3 of the fillets. When the water returns to a boil, lower the heat, cover and simmer for 5 to 7 minutes. The fish should be opaque and firm to the touch at the thickest part. Remove to a warm plate, cover and keep warm while cooking the remaining fish.

Just before serving, reheat the sauce, spoon over each salmon fillet and sprinkle with the rest of the sesame seeds.

Chicken Satay

SERVES 4

I FOUND MANY ADVENTURESOME CHEFS IN SEATTLE playing with Asian flavors and cooking styles, so I was inspired to adapt this recipe from the traditional Thai and Indonesian appetizer that gives it its name. Classic satays, which consist of small strips of marinated chicken, meat or fish, are grilled and served on wooden skewers with various sweet and sour blends of ginger/ peanut/soy dipping sauces. I've turned this into a flavorful main dish that's perfectly accompanied by white or brown rice. The sauce can be made ahead.

2   skinless boneless chicken breasts, halved

2   teaspoons cayenne pepper

1   cup flour

¼   cup peanut oil

2   tablespoons minced gingerroot

1   tablespoon minced garlic

¼   cup minced green onions (white part only)

2   tablespoons sesame oil

1½ cups chicken broth

⅓   cup chunky peanut butter

2   teaspoons hoisin sauce

2   tablespoons soy sauce

1   teaspoon potato starch

2   tablespoons mirin (sweet rice wine)

¼   cup chopped fresh cilantro

Sprinkle the chicken breasts with the cayenne pepper. Place the flour in a wide, shallow dish. Dredge both sides of each half breast in the flour. Shake off any excess. In a large, heavy skillet placed over medium heat, sauté 2 pieces of chicken at a time in the peanut oil for 8 minutes on each side, until they are firm but still springy to the touch. As each piece of chicken is cooked, remove it to a baking pan and place in a warm oven.

In a medium-size, heavy skillet set over medium heat, sauté the ginger, garlic and green onions in the sesame oil for 2 minutes. Using a wire whisk, stir in the chicken broth, peanut butter, hoisin sauce and soy sauce. Bring the sauce to a boil and cook, whisking often, for 10 minutes. Dissolve the potato starch in the mirin and slowly add it to the sauce. Simmer for a couple of minutes, until the sauce thickens.

Cut each half breast across the grain into ½-inch slices. Place on individual plates in a shingled, fan-like shape. Top the chicken with the satay sauce and sprinkle with some of the chopped cilantro.

Fennel Sautéed with Onions and Bacon

SERVES 4

FENNEL IS ONE OF THOSE INTRIGUING vegetables that's enjoying a current rush of popularity, perhaps because it's relatively prolific and because its refreshing taste goes so well with fish. Historically the plant was used for its anise-flavored seeds that provided flavor to meats and greens. Now it's often served thinly sliced in salads or braized on the grill and served as a side dish. In this recipe it is boiled and then tossed with sautéed onion and bacon. It makes an ideal accompaniment for either of the preceding fish recipes.

4 fennel bulbs

3 strips bacon, chopped

1 tablespoon olive oil

1 onion, sliced

1 teaspoon dried oregano

¼ cup chicken broth

1 tablespoon chopped fresh parsley

Remove the stalks and bottom of each fennel bulb. Cut in half lengthwise. Lay each half cut side down and slice across the grain into ½-inch pieces.

Bring a large pot of salted water to a boil. Add the fennel and cook for 7 to 10 minutes, until it is tender.

While the fennel is cooking, cook the bacon in a large, heavy skillet set over medium heat. When it becomes limp and has released some fat, add the olive oil, onion and oregano. Sauté for 5 to 7 minutes, until the bacon is crisp and the onion is beginning to brown.

When the fennel is tender, drain and add to the skillet. Stir to mix the fennel with the onion and bacon. Add the chicken broth, cover and steam for 5 minutes.

Remove with a slotted spoon to individual plates or a serving bowl. Sprinkle with the chopped parsley for color.

Confettied Chard

SERVES 4

ALSO KNOWN AS SWISS CHARD, this green leafy vegetable with stalks that are a pale green or vivid scarlet, first appears in traditional Arabic cooking and has a history that can be traced back to the hanging gardens of Babylon. It's popular around the Mediterranean, particularly in Sicily, southern France and the Catalonia region of Spain. Steamed, cooled, tossed with chopped celery, yellow peppers and carrots and splashed with soy sauce, this dish is big on flavor and very colorful.

1 large bunch chard

3 garlic cloves, minced

¼ cup sliced green onions

2 tablespoons minced gingerroot

2 tablespoons olive oil

½ cup peeled ¼-inch-dice carrots

⅓ cup ¼-inch-dice celery

½ cup seeded ¼-inch-dice yellow bell pepper

⅓ cup chicken broth

2 tablespoons soy sauce

Trim the very ends off the chard stalks and remove any browned edges on the leaves. Chop into 2-inch pieces and soak in a large bowl filled with cold water.

In a deep, heavy pot set over low heat, sauté the garlic, green onions and ginger in the olive oil. Cook for 5 minutes. Raise the heat to medium and add the carrots, celery and yellow pepper. Stir and sauté for 5 minutes.

Lift the chard out of the water and drain in a colander. Place the chard in the pot and pour in the chicken broth and soy sauce. Cover and steam for 3 minutes. Remove the cover, stir and cook for another 3 minutes.

Remove the vegetables using a slotted spoon to individual plates or a serving bowl.

Spiced Apple Bread Pudding

SERVES 10 TO 12

WASHINGTON STATE IS THE NATION'S APPLE KINGDOM, growing more than 60 percent of the country's crop. While Red and Golden Delicious have been the apples of the last century, bred to meet shipping needs and supermarket criteria, today growers are replacing them with new, more flavorful varieties like Braeburn, Gala, Roma, and Fuji. Whatever variety you use in this pudding will soothe and satisfy everyone.

5 large tart apples (such as Granny Smith)

½ teaspoon ground cinnamon

¼ teaspoon ground cloves

¼ teaspoon allspice

Pinch cayenne pepper

½ cup dark brown sugar

½ cup unsalted butter

1 pound stale dense bread (such as French or Italian), cut into 1-inch cubes

⅓ cup dried cranberries

4 eggs plus 2 yolks

4 cups milk

2 teaspoons vanilla extract

Pinch salt

Preheat the oven to 350°F. Peel, core and slice the apples into ½-inch wedges. Place in a large bowl and sprinkle with the cinnamon, cloves, allspice, pepper and 2 tablespoons of the brown sugar. Toss well to coat the apples. Melt 4 tablespoons of the butter in a large skillet over medium heat. Add the apples, cover and cook for 7 minutes, stirring occasionally. The apples should be just slightly cooked, not falling apart. Set aside.

Generously coat a 13 x 9 x 2-inch baking pan with butter. Cover the bottom with the bread. Cover that with a layer of the apple mixture. Sprinkle with the dried cranberries and cover with another layer of bread.

In a medium-size bowl, whisk together the eggs, yolks, milk, remaining brown sugar, vanilla and salt. Carefully pour over the bread and apples. It will take a few minutes to soak in. Melt the remaining 4 tablespoons of butter and pour over the pudding. Place the pan in a larger, deep pan and add 1 inch of hot water to the larger pan. Place on the middle rack of the oven and bake for 60 minutes, until a knife inserted in the center comes out clean. If the pudding has not developed a golden crust on top, place it under the broiler for a couple of minutes until it browns.

Remove from the oven and let rest for 7 to 10 minutes before cutting into serving-size portions.

Napa Valley

Asparagus with Smoked Salmon

Chicken Breasts with
Cabernet Sauce

Pan-Seared Tuna with Herb Butter

Grilled Shrimp with Cilantro
and Toasted Peanuts

Broiled Flank Steak with
Zinfandel Sauce

Artichoke Heart and Potato Gratin

Grilled Polenta with Sautéed
Wild Mushrooms

Champagne Peaches

Frozen Apricot Soufflé with

What does Northern California have that the rest of the Golden State missed out on? Well, it just might be wine style. At least that's my opinion. Drive north of San Francisco and head a little east, then north again on State Highway 29. Skirt the town of Napa and shortly beyond the city limits you enter a wide sunny valley edged with soft golden hills and dotted with dark green live oaks. Welcome to Napa Valley, one of the premier winemaking spots on the earth.

Continuing north, as far as you can see, orderly rows of grapevines march off to the foothills. A sprinkling of mostly low buildings dot the landscape, architectural evidence of the numerous wineries that line the highway all the way to Calistoga and Mt. St. Helena at the end of Napa Valley.

What most people don't realize, and what I was surprised to find out, is that folks have been making wine in California since the early 1800s. Wine was popular during the 1849 gold rush that brought thousands of East Coast fortune seekers to the foothills of the Sierra Nevada Mountains looking for elusive gold nuggets. You might be interested to know that there were just as many acres of grapevines growing in California in 1890 as there were in 1990. Only the vineyards and the varietals have changed.

The other thing I learned about winemaking in Northern California is that this unique coastal valley (as well as a few other areas around the state) offers ideal soil conditions and a perfect microclimate for growing grapes. Warm days that allow the grapes to ripen in the bright sunshine alternate with cool nights that let the color and flavor of the grapes fully develop.

Today the Valley boasts about 45,000 acres planted with various types of grapes and over 200 wineries. No wonder then, that California wines are now ranked among the best in the world, successfully competing with varietals from France, Germany and Italy

With all this winemaking going on, it's only natural that top-notch chefs and food lovers would also gravitate to this part of California. Wine and food have long complimented each other at the dinner table. Enthusiasm for this partnership is an integral part of Napa Valley's cooking traditions as the many excellent restaurants and terrific home cooks here will testify. What I found is that folks here pair wine to sip with various foods, often changing varietals with each course. They also like to cook with wine, adding it to sauces and marinades to enhance flavors and give a subtle richness to the taste of the food. Napa's cooks also insist on using the freshest seasonal ingredients that are generally organic and often available locally in farmers markets—or sometimes right outside the back door in the garden.

Along with seasonal produce like California's own artichokes and asparagus in the spring, apricots and peaches in late summer, you'll find a variety of meat and fresh seafood enjoyed here as well. These foods are prepared simply by grilling, roasting or pan searing to highlight their unique tastes. The result is a distinctive cooking style that's light, flavorful and unfailingly satisfying. I know you'll agree when you try my selection of recipes featuring Northern California's delicious wine style.

Asparagus with Smoked Salmon

SERVES 4 TO 6

EVERY SPRING, ON A SEASONAL QUEST for the best and the freshest ingredients, Napa Valley's chefs keep an eye open for the first tender, green asparagus shoots to arrive in local markets. Few realize they're echoing a custom that cooks have followed since ancient times when Romans and Syrians cultivated asparagus in their home gardens. Now grown extensively in California, Washington State and Mexico, asparagus growers must wait patiently for two years before hand harvesting the tips of the plants, one reason this vegetable is expensive.

2 pounds thin asparagus

8 ounces smoked salmon, thinly sliced

2 tablespoons chopped fresh dill

Freshly ground pepper to taste

Trim the ends off the asparagus spears. Bring a pot, large enough to accommodate the length of the asparagus, filled with 4 inches of water to a boil over high heat. Add the asparagus and blanch for 5 to 7 minutes, until it is tender but not soggy. Drain and rinse under cold water to stop the cooking. Place the asparagus flat on paper towels to dry.

Roll a slice of smoked salmon on a diagonal around each asparagus spear. Spread the fresh dill on a plate. Grind the pepper over the dill. Roll each asparagus spear in the mixture, pressing down lightly so the pepper and dill will stick.

Cover and refrigerate until ready to serve.

Chicken Breasts with Cabernet Sauce

SERVES 4

COOKING WITH WINE IS A given in the cuisine of this part of northern California, where wineries line the main highway headed north and vineyards form a tight patchwork across the valley floor. Wine adds a richness to sauces and marinades that complements many ingredients, particularly meat and poultry. The first rule is that the wine, whatever its color, must be smooth and not harsh, although it does not have to be a "great" wine to achieve the desired taste.

2 large skinless boneless chicken breasts, halved

1 teaspoon salt

1 teaspoon freshly ground pepper

1 cup flour

4 tablespoons unsalted butter

1 tablespoon olive oil

2 cups Cabernet Sauvignon

2 teaspoons minced shallots

1 teaspoon dried sage

1 cup chicken broth

1 tablespoon tomato paste

On a sturdy surface, pound the thickest part of each breast with a meat mallet. Sprinkle both sides with the salt and pepper. Dredge the chicken in the flour, shaking off any excess.

In a wide, heavy skillet placed over medium heat, melt 1 tablespoon of the butter in the olive oil. Sauté 2 pieces of chicken at a time for 8 minutes on each side, until they are slightly firm. As each piece of chicken is cooked, remove to a baking pan and place in a warm oven.

When the chicken is sautéed, bring the Cabernet Sauvignon, shallots and sage to a boil in the skillet. Boil until it has reduced to a few tablespoons, about 5 to 7 minutes. Strain through a fine-mesh sieve into a small pot and return to the heat. Add the chicken broth and tomato paste. Whisk to incorporate the paste and boil for another 5 minutes, until the sauce has reduced to ¾ cup. Remove the pot from the heat and swirl in the remaining butter, a tablespoon at a time, adding a new piece as the last one dissolves.

Cut each half breast across the grain into ½-inch slices. Place on individual plates in a shingled, fan-like shape. Spoon with some sauce and serve.

Napa Valley

Pan-Seared Tuna with Herb Butter

SERVES 6

I LOVE THE DENSE MEATY TEXTURE OF TUNA, a result of the strong muscles this magnificent fish needs to swim constantly and maintain an adequate oxygen supply. Find the freshest fish with clear eyes (if whole), a clean-looking skin with no missing scales (which could indicate age or improper handling), and no fishy smell. Fresh tuna also has deep red flesh. The simple preparation offered here, the use of fresh ingredients (California-style) and the herb butter all enhance the tuna's rich taste.

- 8 tablespoons unsalted butter, softened
- 2 tablespoons finely chopped fresh parsley
- 2 garlic cloves, minced
- 2 tablespoons chopped fresh chives
- 1½ pounds fresh tuna, cut into six 1-inch-thick slices
- 1 tablespoon coarse salt
- 2 teaspoons freshly ground pepper
- 1 teaspoon cayenne pepper
- ⅓ cup olive oil

In a small bowl, using a rubber spatula, mix together the butter, parsley, garlic and chives. Place a 10 x 10-inch piece of plastic wrap on a flat surface. Scrape the butter mixture into a log shape, 6 inches long and 2 inches from the bottom edge of the plastic sheet. Fold the short end of the plastic over the butter and roll the log to the other edge of the sheet. Hold the plastic at the ends and roll it several times to give it a smooth, round shape. Fold the ends under the log, place on a plate and refrigerate for at least an hour.

Place the tuna in a shallow roasting pan and sprinkle both sides with the salt, pepper and cayenne. Coat with the olive oil. Cover and refrigerate for 30 minutes.

Place a large, heavy skillet over high heat for 3 to 5 minutes. Sprinkle a few drops of water into the pan. If they jump and evaporate quickly, it is hot enough to start cooking. Place as many of the tuna steaks in the pan as you can without letting them touch and cook for 5 minutes on each side. The steaks should be well browned and crisp on the outside and rare to medium on the inside.

Place each steak on a plate or serving platter. Cut the butter into ¾-inch slices and place one on each steak. Serve immediately.

Grilled Shrimp with Cilantro and Toasted Peanuts

SERVES 4 TO 6

LIKE SEATTLE, CALIFORNIA COOKS have discovered Pacific Rim flavors too, as this grilled shrimp recipe with cilantro and peanuts testifies. Prepared in a flash, it's an easy appetizer or main course with the marinated shrimp picking up flavor and texture from the crunchy peanuts and pungent cilantro. If you're using a charcoal grill, check to make sure the coals are red-hot with just a thin layer of ash on their surface for medium-high heat. Test by holding your hand about six inches from the surface of the grill. If you can only hold it there for a few seconds, it's ready for you to put on the shrimp.

24	medium shrimp
1	tablespoon fresh lime juice
2	garlic cloves, minced
½	cup chopped fresh cilantro
½	cup olive oil
⅔	cup finely chopped salted peanuts

Peel shrimp, leaving the tails on. Remove the veins and rinse well under cool water. Pat dry with paper towels and place in a medium-size bowl. Sprinkle with the lime juice, garlic and ¼ cup of the chopped cilantro. Toss well. Add the olive oil, toss, cover and refrigerate for 20 minutes.

Preheat the oven to 475°F. Spread the chopped peanuts evenly on a baking sheet and bake for 7 to 10 minutes, until they begin to brown. Immediately remove from the pan to a small bowl. Add the remaining cilantro, toss well and set aside.

Bring the grill to medium-high heat. Thread 4 to 6 shrimp onto metal or wooden skewers and grill for 2 to 3 minutes on each side until bright pink and cooked through. Remove to a serving platter or individual plates and sprinkle generously with the peanut mixture. Serve immediately.

Broiled Flank Steak with Zinfandel Sauce

SERVES 4 TO 6

THE WORD "STEAK" COMES FROM an Old Norse word meaning "to roast on a spit," a common method of meat cookery in England since Viking times. The name remains to describe one of the most popular forms of eating beef. Most contemporary preparations of steak involve a fast grilling of the meat under high heat to the desired degree of "doneness." Using a hearty Zinfandel to make a tenderizing marinade Wine Country-style, adds a rich flavor accent to the meat.

1   2-pound flank steak

1   tablespoon freshly ground pepper

2   tablespoons olive oil

1   cup red Zinfandel wine

2   garlic cloves, minced

2   tablespoons minced shallots

½   teaspoon salt

2   cups veal or chicken broth

4   tablespoons unsalted butter, room temperature

Place the flank steak in a roasting pan and sprinkle both sides with the pepper. Press the pepper into the steak. Rub the olive oil on both sides. In a small mixing bowl or measuring cup, stir together the wine, garlic and shallots. Pour over the steak. Turn the steak so the marinade covers both sides. Cover and refrigerate for 2 hours. Turn the steak every 30 minutes.

Preheat the broiler. Lift the steak out of the marinade and place on a broiling pan or a metal rack placed in a shallow roasting pan. Broil 3 inches from the heat for 4 minutes. Turn the steak and broil for another 4 minutes. Remove the steak to a carving board, sprinkle with the salt and allow to rest in a warm spot for 5 minutes.

While the steak is resting, make the sauce. Pour the marinade into a small saucepot. Bring to a boil over high heat. Add the broth and any juices that have collected on the carving board, and continue to boil for another 5 minutes, or until the sauce has reduced to about ½ cup. Turn off the heat and add the butter, about 1 tablespoon at a time, swirling until each piece has dissolved before adding another.

Thinly slice the steak on a bias across its grain. Ladle a few spoonfuls of sauce over each portion and pour the remainder into a warmed bowl to serve.

Artichoke Heart and Potato Gratin

SERVES 6

CALIFORNIA IS THE ARTICHOKE CAPITAL of the world, with acres of the spreading gray-green plants flourishing all over the Monterey Peninsula. Did you know that the artichoke is actually a member of the thistle family and the part we eat is the plant's flower if allowed to bloom? The prickly thistle is mainly the faintly purple "choke" that we scoop out when eating fresh, steamed artichokes. But you won't have that chore with this recipe, just that unique artichoke taste. It accents the potatoes in this sophisticated side dish that's a delicious variation on the classic potatoes au gratin.

1½	pounds Yukon Gold or russet potatoes, peeled, sliced ⅛-inch-thick
1	teaspoon salt
3	tablespoons unsalted butter, softened
2	garlic cloves, minced
2	medium onions, thinly sliced
1	red bell pepper, seeded, thinly sliced
1	14¾-ounce can artichoke hearts, drained, diced
½	teaspoon oregano
1	cup heavy cream

Spread the potato slices in a wide skillet and sprinkle them with ½ teaspoon of the salt. Cover with an inch of water and bring to a boil over high heat. As soon as it boils, drain, reserving the cooking water for later.

Preheat the oven to 325°F.

Coat a 2-quart, 14 x 8 x 2-inch glass or enamel baking pan (aluminum will react with the artichokes) with 1 tablespoon of the butter. Scatter the minced garlic over the bottom. Layer the potatoes, onions, red pepper and diced artichoke hearts evenly in the pan. Sprinkle with the remaining salt and the oregano. Dot with the remaining butter and pour the cream and 1 cup of the reserved cooking liquid over the top.

Bake the gratin for 1½ hours, until the potatoes are tender and a golden crust has formed over the top.

Grilled Polenta with Sautéed Wild Mushrooms

SERVES 6 TO 8

POLENTA, THAT THICK, COZY PORRIDGE made from simmered cornmeal, has become a staple in California cuisine because its mild flavor compliments so many entrées. Polenta originated in northern Italy and both Venice and the Lombardy region claim ownership. Culinary historians know Venetians visiting from America introduced maize (corn) to Italy in the mid-1600s. In the U.S., polenta's popularity means it's readily available in most grocery stores. Look for the solid polenta "logs," prepared and ready to slice, to make this grilled version with flavorful mushrooms that's scrumptious served with poultry, meat or fish.

3 tablespoons olive oil

1 tablespoon unsalted butter

2 garlic cloves, minced

½ cup minced shallots

4 ounces shiitake mushrooms, stems removed, sliced

4 ounces oyster mushrooms, sliced

4 ounces crimini mushrooms, sliced

1 24-ounce package prepared polenta

¼ cup red wine

1 teaspoon salt

½ teaspoon freshly ground pepper

In a wide, heavy skillet, heat 2 tablespoons of the olive oil and the butter over medium heat. When the butter has melted, add the garlic and shallots. Stir and cook for 3 minutes. Add the mushrooms, stir well and sauté for 7 to 10 minutes. When the mushrooms are soft and most of the moisture has evaporated, remove from the heat and set aside while you grill the polenta.

Bring the grill to medium heat. Cut the polenta into 8 rounds and brush both sides with the remaining olive oil. Grill until heated through, about 3 minutes per side. Remove and place a round on each plate.

Return the mushrooms to high heat and add the red wine. When the mixture begins to bubble, adjust with the salt and pepper and spoon over the polenta. Serve immediately.

Champagne Peaches

SERVES 4

I'VE DISCOVERED THAT the secret to truly enjoying peaches is to eat them. Immediately! When selecting peaches note that there are two types: freestone and clingstone, a notation that indicates how the fruit's flesh pulls away from the stone. Odds are that your peaches will be from California since that state produces 50 percent of those sold in the United States. Choose peaches carefully and make sure they are ripe—they'll have a gentle "give" around the stem area plus that unmistakable sweet fragrance—with an unblemished surface when you buy them. Then eat them within 48 hours, or make some decadent dessert that celebrates their glory.

4 large ripe peaches, peeled, pitted, cut into ½-inch slices

1 tablespoon lemon juice

3 tablespoons unsalted butter

1 tablespoon brown sugar

Pinch ground cloves

2 cups champagne

Place the peach slices in a large mixing bowl and toss them with the lemon juice. Melt the butter in a large, heavy skillet set over high heat. As soon as the butter begins to bubble, add the peaches. Sprinkle them with the brown sugar and cloves. Sauté, turning and shaking the slices until they are lightly browned on the edges, about 5 to 7 minutes. Add the champagne and cook until the champagne has reduced to a cup.

Serve warm over ice cream, a slice of cake or with a dollop of sour cream.

Frozen Apricot Soufflé

SERVES 12

IF YOU'RE LUCKY ENOUGH to taste a fresh-picked apricot, warmed by California sunshine, there are few fruits more delectable. Although tender-skinned apricots are not good travelers, more and more are making their way into markets far from their West Coast habitat. Apricots first grew wild in China, then were cultivated in India and Persia. Used most often in desserts and sweet dishes, they provide this chilled soufflé's delicate summer flavor.

SOUFFLÉ

- 1   1¼-ounce envelope unflavored gelatin
- ¼   teaspoon ground cinnamon
- ½   cup evaporated skim milk
- ½   cup light brown sugar
- 2   cups vanilla yogurt
- ½   cup light corn syrup
- 2   cups peeled diced fresh apricots (about 1 pound)
- 8   ounces heavy cream

SAUCE

- 1   16-ounce bag frozen raspberries, thawed
- 2   tablespoons lemon juice
- 1   tablespoon honey
- 2   teaspoons arrowroot

FOR SOUFFLÉ: Whisk together the gelatin, cinnamon and skim milk in a small pot. Let stand for 2 minutes to soften the gelatin. Place over medium heat and stir until the gelatin is dissolved. Add the brown sugar, yogurt and corn syrup. Remove from the heat.

Puree the apricots in a food processor until they are smooth. Combine with the gelatin mixture, pour into a 9 x 11 x 2-inch pan and freeze until almost solid, about an hour.

In a large mixing bowl, beat the heavy cream until stiff. When the apricot base is frozen, beat with an electric mixer on low speed for 30 seconds and then for 2 minutes on high.

Fold the apricot base into the whipped cream until blended. Pour into a 2-quart soufflé dish and freeze for about 2 hours, or until firm.

FOR SAUCE: Empty the thawed raspberries into a fine-mesh strainer set over a small pot. Press the raspberries to release all of their juices. Discard the seeds. Stir in the remaining ingredients and bring to a gentle boil over medium heat. Remove from the heat when slightly thickened. Serve the soufflé with the raspberry sauce.

NEW ENGLAND

Baked Clams with Bacon

New England Clam Chowder

Chicken Pot Pie

Lobster Roll

Bay Scallops in White Wine Sauce

Cranberry Succotash

Steamed Brown Bread

Pumpkin Pie

Boston Cream Pie

Walking around seacoast towns in New England, from Connecticut to Maine, I feel like I've stepped back in time—narrow cobblestone streets shaded by leafy trees, sturdy 18th and 19th century houses looking out to sea, and always a harbor filled with boats. Over the centuries, their protected settings and close proximity to rich North Atlantic fishing grounds made these towns the focus of New England's successful fishing industry. Some have relinquished this colorful past, but others struggle on today, although beset by over-fishing and government regulations. Still others are enjoying a renaissance, paticularly in Maine, where the lobstering business is booming from an abundance of the clawed crustaceans. Either way, New England's past and present seafarers are proud of their heritage.

As a result, I can tell you that generations of New England men have gone down to sea and plied rough, cold Atlantic waters in search of herring, cod and mackerel, or built and sailed majestic ships to distant foreign ports. Despite the ocean's lure and promise of adventure, the recent best-selling book and movie, The Perfect Storm, made the risks of being a fisherman abundantly clear. It's not an easy life.

Just as the sea gets in one's blood here and colors the history of many New England coastal towns, it also, naturally, plays a big role in the region's culinary traditions. Here, what you catch from the ocean is very often what you eat. New England colonists lived in a harsh climate and didn't have an easy time scratching out a living from the rugged coast where they settled, either on land or at sea. Add to this Puritan values that stressed making do with limited means, thriftiness, and laboring "for the common good." These attitudes also restricted thinking about food. I wasn't too surprised to find out that the first New England cookbooks were written to outline domestic principles and good manners—interpreted as good morals—rather than to celebrate the pleasures of the table. If New England cooking is considered plain with no frills, that's why.

Still, New England cooking has a generous measure of delicious, hearty chowders and stews, down-to-earth breads, and no-nonsense vegetable side dishes. As a reward for all their appetite-building hard work, fishermen and sailors indeed ate well. A bounty of seafood from tidal flats and the ocean made up their meals and anchored the region's straightforward traditional cuisine that also includes simple fare like beans and grains. Add a wholesome pumpkin pie delicately seasoned with cinnamon and nutmeg and life is good.

In discovering and tasting these dishes, I also have to mention that I ran into a lot of passionate cooks in this part of the world who love the region's traditional dishes and will argue for hours about what makes a "real" jonnycake or "true" clam chowder. New Englanders do love their food. You'll discover what they know and what I learned: that there are indeed many pleasures on the New England table. I invite you to taste what I think are the best of the region's classic dishes.

Baked Clams with Bacon

SERVES 4 TO 6

BELIEVE IT OR NOT, CLAMS WERE originally considered fish bait. Not until the late 1800s did clams achieve their current status as a delicacy from the sea, but even then clam digs were localized and the booty most often enjoyed at shore picnics. When selecting clams, reject any open shells and rinse them well of mud and grit under cold running water, or let them soak for a half an hour in cold water sprinkled with a little cornmeal so they disgorge themselves. Melted butter and possibly cocktail sauce are traditional accompaniments for eating clams, but this recipe offers a delicious twist on those classics.

Rice, enough for an inch on bottom of two 9 x 13 x 2-inch baking pans

2 dozen littleneck clams on the half shell

1 cup butter, room temperature

¼ cup minced shallots

¼ cup minced fresh parsley

1 tablespoon white wine

6 slices bacon, coarsely chopped

Freshly ground pepper to taste

Preheat the oven to 450°F. Fill the baking pans with the rice until they are covered with a 1-inch layer. Nestle the clams securely in the rice. This will prevent them from tipping.

In a small bowl, combine the butter, shallots, parsley and white wine. Place a dab of this compound butter on each clam.

Sauté the bacon over medium heat for 5 to 7 minutes in a large, heavy skillet. When it is browned, lift out the pieces with a slotted spoon and drain on paper towels. When cool enough to handle, place a large pinch of bacon on each clam. Sprinkle the clams with the freshly ground pepper.

Bake the clams, uncovered, for 5 to 7 minutes, until the bacon is crisp.

New England Clam Chowder

SERVES 6 TO 8

THERE ARE AS MANY VERSIONS OF THIS hearty chowder on the New England coast as there are cooks. What began as an event in the 1800s with festive chowder parties and outdoor picnics continues today with this glorious seafood "stew" that can be eaten as a starter or as a whole meal. Original recipes called for white-fleshed fish (fresh preferred), salt pork for flavor and richness, hard biscuits or bread to thicken the broth, and water. Onions, potatoes and milk were optional, but became standard by the 1880s. But heaven forbid a chowder contain tomatoes or other common soup vegetables like celery or carrots!

1 quart clams with their juice

2 cups water

2 slices bacon, chopped

1 medium onion, diced

3 cups peeled ½-inch-cubed potatoes

3 tablespoons unsalted butter, room temperature

2 cups half-and-half

2 teaspoons salt

½ teaspoon white pepper

Oyster crackers

Place the clams, juice and water in a large pot set over medium heat. When it comes to a boil, drain into a large bowl, reserving the broth. Chop the clams, removing any tough membranes. Set aside.

In a deep, heavy pot, sauté the bacon over medium heat until browned, about 5 minutes. Add the onion and cook for 5 more minutes until it is translucent and limp. Pour in the clam broth and potatoes. Simmer for 12 to 15 minutes, until the potatoes are tender. Stir in the butter, half-and-half, salt, white pepper and the chopped clams. Heat through, but do not allow to boil.

Serve immediately with oyster crackers.

Chicken Pot Pie

SERVES 6 TO 8

THIS IS MY IDEA OF PERFECT COMFORT FOOD: moist chicken pieces and bright peas and carrots in a creamy, herb-flavored sauce bubbling under a flaky crust of buttery puff pastry. The first pot pie was probably created by an enterprising New Englander who borrowed the concept of meat-filled pies, indigenous to the cuisines of England, France and Germany, from his or her European ancestors. No doubt thrifty, that New Englander also realized that they could get extra mileage out of leftover chicken and vegetables by making savory, one-dish pies.

6 tablespoons unsalted butter

6 tablespoons flour

1 cup milk

2 cups chicken stock

½ teaspoon rosemary

½ teaspoon sage

2 green onions, sliced

1 teaspoon salt

1 teaspoon freshly ground pepper

4 cups bite-size pieces cooked chicken

2 cups frozen peas, thawed

2 cups sliced cooked carrots

1 frozen puff pastry sheet, thawed

1 egg yolk

1 tablespoon water

Melt the butter in a large, heavy skillet over medium heat. Stir in the flour and cook the roux, stirring often, until it softens and looks as if it is melting, about 5 to 7 minutes. Using a wire whisk, slowly add the milk and chicken stock. Stir slowly until the sauce thickens. Add the rosemary, sage, green onions, salt and pepper and cook for 3 minutes.

Preheat the oven to 425°F.

Spread the chicken on the bottom of a 2½-quart casserole dish. Sprinkle with the peas and carrots. Pour the sauce over the chicken. Place the puff pastry over the top of the casserole. With wet fingers, crimp the pastry onto the edge of the casserole. Using a sharp knife, make several slits in the pastry as vents. In a small bowl, mix together the egg yolk and water. Brush over the pastry, place the pot pie in the oven and bake for 30 to 40 minutes, until browned and bubbling.

Lobster Roll

SERVES 8

YOU CAN'T DRIVE UP AND DOWN the New England coast without seeing numerous signs offering one of the region's most famous foods—the lobster roll. But if you're lucky and have time to drive off the beaten path, you may find a local clam shack on the edge of a tidal creek touting its homemade version of lobster rolls. I'd advise stopping to check them out. These days there is an abundance of the cold water critters and no one really knows why, but that leaves plenty of sweet lobster to be enjoyed in this favorite summer sandwich on an afternoon when all you have to do is watch the tide go in and out.

8 frankfurter buns

¼ cup unsalted butter, melted

1 cup mayonnaise

½ teaspoon salt

2 tablespoons minced fresh basil

2 green onions, thinly sliced

1 tablespoon lemon juice

1 teaspoon freshly ground pepper

3 cups cooked lobster meat (about 2 pounds), cut into bite-size pieces

Paprika

Preheat the oven to 400°F.

Open the frankfurter buns and place them split side up on a baking sheet. Brush them with the butter and bake until light brown. Remove from the oven and set aside.

Whisk together the mayonnaise, salt, basil, green onions, lemon juice and pepper in a small bowl. Place the lobster meat in a large bowl and add the mayonnaise mixture. Toss to coat the lobster meat well.

Spoon the lobster mixture into the frankfurter buns. Sprinkle with the paprika and serve.

Bay Scallops in White Wine Sauce

SERVES 4 TO 6

LIKE CLAMS, SCALLOPS WERE ONCE low on the list of desirable shellfish. In fact, New England cookbooks didn't regularly reference scallops until the 1870s, and even then people were puzzled by their sweet flavor and uncertain about how to prepare them. My, how that has changed! These bivalves, harvested from November to April either by individual divers or by commercial draggers, are very popular on menus now and small bay scallops are the most prized—and most expensive. This simple preparation in a white wine sauce allows the full richness of the delicate scallop flavor to come forth.

2 pounds bay scallops

⅔ cup unsalted butter, softened

2 tablespoons minced shallots

1 tablespoon minced fresh parsley

Juice of ½ lemon

1 cup dry white wine

1 bay leaf

Salt to taste

Rinse the scallops and pat them dry with paper towels.

Melt half of the butter in a large, heavy skillet over medium heat. Add the shallots and cook for 3 to 5 minutes. Raise the heat to high and add the scallops. Sauté for 3 to 5 minutes, until they begin to brown. Sprinkle with the parsley and remove from the pan with a slotted spoon to a warm pan. Squeeze the lemon over the scallops and keep warm.

Pour the white wine into the skillet and add the bay leaf. Bring to a boil over high heat. Boil for 2 to 4 minutes, until it has reduced by about ⅓. Lower the heat until the wine just simmers and swirl in small pieces of the remaining softened butter. Add more butter only as the preceding pieces have melted. Continue to swirl the sauce. Do not allow the sauce to boil. Continue until all the butter is incorporated. Stir in any juices that may have been released by the scallops into the sauce. Remove the bay leaf and adjust the seasoning with salt.

Place equal portions of the scallops onto the center of each plate. Spoon the sauce over the scallops and serve immediately.

Cranberry Succotash

SERVES 4 TO 6

THIS MAY BE ONE OF THE MOST AUTHENTIC *New England dishes on record since "succotash" is formed from Narragansett Indian words. The Narragansett tribe inhabited the place we know today as Rhode Island. While the dish always requires corn kernels and lima beans, and early versions included salt pork, there are dozens of ways to make it, including the version here with cranberries, another ingredient native to New England. Originally served as a summertime side dish, frozen vegetables make it possible to enjoy succotash year-round.*

2 cups fresh baby lima beans or frozen, thawed

2 strips bacon, finely chopped

1 cup diced onions

2 cups fresh or frozen corn kernels

½ cup chopped frozen cranberries

1 cup light cream

1 teaspoon salt

Place the lima beans in a medium-size pot and cover with water. Over medium-high heat, bring the beans to a boil. Strain, reserving some of the liquid, and set aside. Omit this step if using frozen lima beans.

In a deep, heavy pot, cook the bacon over medium heat until it becomes limp, about 3 to 5 minutes. Stir in the onions and corn and continue to cook for another 5 to 7 minutes, until they begin to brown. Add the lima beans, cranberries, light cream and salt. Bring to a simmer. Stir often and cook for 10 minutes, until the beans are soft. If too much liquid evaporates, add a little more cream, or blanching water, or some chicken or vegetable broth.

Spoon onto plates and serve immediately.

Steamed Brown Bread

MAKES 2 LOAVES

THIS IS ONE OF THOSE NEW ENGLAND CULINARY treats that defies attempts to trace its recipe genealogy. But by most accounts, the recipe for classic steamed brown bread seems to be derived from a "rye and Indian" bread that was adapted mid-19th century to become a steamed bread. In that version, molasses and milk were added to the traditional recipe ingredients and a quick-rising agent replaced the yeast. For whatever reason, coffee cans or all-metal shortening cans have long been used as baking pans. Be sure to eat this bread warm, in round slices slathered with butter.

¾ cup sifted flour

¾ cup cornmeal

1 cup whole wheat flour

¾ cup rye flour

1 teaspoon baking soda

1 teaspoon baking powder

Pinch ground cloves

1 teaspoon salt

¾ cup dark molasses

1½ cups buttermilk

1 cup minced raisins

Coat the insides of two 13-ounce coffee cans with vegetable shortening. Place a circle of waxed paper in the bottom of each can.

In a large mixing bowl, whisk together the dry ingredients. Stir in the molasses, buttermilk and raisins until a batter is formed. Pour into the prepared cans. They should be only ⅔ full. Cover with pieces of aluminum foil that have been coated with shortening. Tie securely with cotton string.

Place a rack on the bottom of a deep, heavy pot. Place the cans in the pot. Add enough boiling water to come halfway up the cans. Cover and steam for 1 hour.

When a metal skewer inserted in the center of each loaf comes out clean, lift the cans out of the pot and let them cool for a few minutes on a wire rack. Remove the foil and gently ease the bread from the cans. When the bread is just warm, cut ¼-inch slices and serve.

Pumpkin Pie

SERVES 8

FOR EARLY NEW ENGLANDERS, THANKSGIVING WAS *celebrated in the style of a traditional English autumn harvest feast long before it became a national holiday. Proclaimed by the local minister, the occasion was even more of a holiday than Christmas and everyone got involved in the preparations, including making at least three kinds of pies. Although English recipes dating to the 17th and 18th centuries exist for pumpkin pie, the dish might have originated in Italy and migrated northward, finally coming to the New World with the first colonists. Whatever its derivation, this subtly spiced, custardy pie is a perennial favorite.*

2 cups pumpkin puree

1 cup cottage cheese

½ teaspoon ground ginger

½ teaspoon ground cinnamon

¼ teaspoon ground cloves

1 teaspoon salt

½ cup sour cream

2 eggs, lightly beaten

⅓ cup brandy

1 9-inch unbaked pie shell

Preheat the oven to 450°F.

Place the pumpkin puree, cottage cheese, ginger, cinnamon, cloves, salt and sour cream in the bowl of a food processor. Puree until very smooth. Pour into a large mixing bowl.

In a small bowl, whisk together the eggs and brandy. Slowly mix into the pumpkin mixture. Pour into the pie shell.

Bake the pie for 10 minutes, then reduce the heat to 350°F and bake for another 30 minutes. Remove to a wire rack and let cool completely.

New England

Boston Cream Pie

SERVES 8 TO 10

DON'T LET THE NAME FOOL YOU. *This is not really a pie at all, but an airy yellow layer cake with a creamy custard filling and a shiny chocolate glaze frosting masquerading as a pie. According to* The Dictionary of American Food & Drink, *the first printed mention of this dessert was in 1855 in* The New York Herald. *When Boston's Parker House hotel opened in 1856, it appeared on the menu as Parker House Chocolate Pie. Served chilled, this cake was a special one made for formal occasions and church suppers.*

⅓ cup unsalted butter

1 cup sugar

1 egg

2 cups sifted cake flour

1 tablespoon baking powder

½ teaspoon salt

¾ cup milk

1 teaspoon vanilla extract

2 6-ounce packages vanilla pudding mix

2 cups heavy cream

12 ounces semisweet chocolate, chopped

Using an electric mixer on high speed, beat the butter with the sugar until light and fluffy. Beat in the egg.

Sift the flour, baking powder and salt into a small bowl. With the mixer on low speed, spoon the flour into the butter mixture, alternating with the milk and vanilla. When the batter is smooth, pour into 2 buttered and floured 8-inch pans and bake for 25 minutes, or until the center of the cake is springy to the touch. Cool the pans on a rack for 5 minutes before turning out to finish cooling.

Prepare the pudding according to the manufacturer's directions. Beat 1 cup of the heavy cream until stiff and fold it into the pudding.

In a small pot placed over medium heat, bring the remaining cream to a boil. Immediately remove from the heat and whisk in the chocolate until it is slightly thickened and cooled.

Center one cake layer on a serving plate. Spread the filling evenly over it and top with the other cake layer. Gently press down until the filling can just be seen. Pour the chocolate icing over the top of the cake. Chill in the refrigerator for 30 minutes before serving.

MID-ATLANTIC

Curried Crab Cakes

Chicken and Corn Soup

Glazed Baked Ham

Roast Duck with Red Cabbage

Free-Range Turkey with Port Sauce

Potatoes and Sugar Snap Peas

Shoofly Pie

Gingerbread

I first visited the Chesapeake Bay with my family as a young boy. I was enchanted then—and still am today—by its beauty. I also distinctly remember eating some terrific food, which was a given when you grow up in a family of great cooks spending a week at the shore. But there was also a delicious variety of local ingredients to cook with, all native to this great estuary region that spans three states and ranges two hundred miles in length, and I'm sure that inspired them, too.

So many delicious ingredients close at hand on sea and shore led the area's first European settlers to develop a provincial cooking style that's one of the oldest of our country's regional cuisines. The preparation is simple and uncontrived, and uses the freshest ingredients possible. As a result, recipes and cooking methods in this region tend to be handed down between generations and prepared from personal memories rather than cookbooks.

More often than not, you'll find traditional dishes of the Mid-Atlantic region prepared in one pot, whether it's a savory chicken corn soup, a venison stew, or a baked Smithfield ham. You see, colonial cooking involved open fires on a hearth and was a challenge. One-pot cooking helped keep things under control. Today's locals, being practical folk, figure there's no need to change cooking methods just because electric and gas stoves have replaced fireplaces—particularly when the results are so tasty—and so the tradition lives on.

Of course, the first thing most people think of when you mention the Chesapeake Bay is seafood. With good reason! There's a wealth of oysters, clams and that prince of crustaceans, the blue crab, that make their home in the waters of the Chesapeake and its tributaries, and support its prosperous seafood industry. From late May through the first months of Autumn, everyone here eats anything crab with great gusto, and these eating occasions often serve as the basis for family feasts and community social events.

Along with the Chesapeake Bay's seafood offerings, early settlers found the surrounding marshes and woodlands flush with waterfowl and game every Autumn. This inspired a sporting tradition of hunting and serving wild duck, goose and venison that continues today.

European colonists contributed their culinary traditions (red cabbage, prosciutto, cheeses) to those already thriving here. In addition, they also cleared forests for farms and from New Jersey and Pennsylvania down through Delaware and Maryland into coastal Virginia, there are fertile farmlands that grow all sorts of produce—from lettuces and berries to tomatoes, sweet corn, peas and squash and more. The area is also one of the largest producers of country ham—pork that's been cured and smoked—particularly Smithfield hams from the region of the same name on the James River in Virginia. These are the superstars of the ham world and my favorite, too.

With the recipes on the next pages, it's my pleasure to introduce you to the delicious fare of the Chesapeake Bay and the Mid-Atlantic coast. I hope you enjoy the feast.

Curried Crab Cakes

SERVES 8 AS AN APPETIZER, 4 AS AN ENTRÉE

ALL ALONG THE EASTERN SEABOARD, Atlantic blue crabs are a delicacy relished in summertime. But nowhere are the crabs as plentiful or celebrated as in the Chesapeake Bay region. In fact, in Baltimore and all along Maryland's Eastern Shore, crab cakes and crab feasts are as integral to the regional culture as the rise and fall of the tide. Every family, it seems, has its own crab cakes recipe, often secretly guarded. But you won't go wrong with the one here. Buy lump crabmeat ready to use, or crack your own cooked crabs and pick out the moist, succulent crabmeat.

2 pounds lump crabmeat, drained, picked over

¼ cup mayonnaise

1 teaspoon salt

⅔ cup sliced green onions

2 eggs, beaten

3 tablespoons curry powder

⅔ cup fresh breadcrumbs

2 cups mayonnaise

1 teaspoon salt

1 teaspoon freshly ground pepper

2 tablespoons extra-virgin olive oil

½ cup chopped fresh cilantro

2 to 3 drops hot pepper sauce (such as Tabasco)

½ cup peanut oil

1 cup flour

In a large mixing bowl, gently combine the crabmeat with the mayonnaise, salt, green onions, eggs, 2 tablespoons of the curry powder and enough breadcrumbs to just bind. Form into 8 cakes and place on a baking sheet. Cover and refrigerate for at least 30 minutes.

While the crab cakes are chilling, prepare the cilantro mayonnaise. Place the mayonnaise, salt, pepper, olive oil, cilantro and hot sauce in a food processor. Puree until well combined. Remove to a small bowl. Cover and chill until ready to serve.

Heat the peanut oil in a large, heavy skillet over medium-high heat. In a wide, shallow bowl, combine the flour with the remaining curry powder. Dredge the crab cakes in the flour mixture and immediately fry in the hot oil. Cook 2 or 3 at a time for 5 minutes. Gently turn over and cook for another 5 minutes. If they are browning too quickly, adjust the heat accordingly. When cooked, remove to paper towels to drain and then place on a warm plate and cover until they are all done.

Serve with a small bowl of the cilantro mayonnaise for each plate.

Chicken and Corn Soup

SERVES 4 TO 6

CORN WAS GROWING IN THE NEW WORLD long before the first European colonists arrived on the Atlantic Coast. In fact, evidence indicates that maize, the ancestor of our modern sweet corn, was probably being harvested in Peru around 1000 B.C. As people traveled from region to region, corn moved into North America and became a staple food for Native Americans who cultivated it in their gardens. They, in turn, introduced corn to the first colonists who might not have survived without it. To celebrate this legacy of corn in our culinary heritage, try this hearty soup. If fresh corn is not available, frozen corn works well, too.

1   cup fresh corn kernels or frozen, thawed

2   tablespoons unsalted butter

½   cup diced onion

2   tablespoons olive oil

¼   teaspoon marjoram

½   teaspoon basil

4   cups chicken broth

2   cups diced cooked chicken

2   tablespoons chopped fresh basil, green onions or chives

Salt to taste

In a heavy deep pot set over medium heat, sauté ½ cup of the corn kernels in the butter for 3 to 5 minutes, until they are bright yellow and slightly soft. Place the corn in a blender or food processor and puree until smooth. Strain through a fine sieve into a small bowl. Press hard on the solids to squeeze out all the liquid.

Sauté the onion in the olive oil over low heat in the pot used for the corn. When the onion is limp, after about 3 to 5 minutes, add the herbs and cook for another 2 minutes. Add the chicken broth and corn puree, and raise the heat to high. When the soup comes to a boil, lower the heat until it simmers and cook for 15 minutes, until it has reduced to about 3 cups and is slightly thickened. The soup can be prepared ahead up to this point and refrigerated when cooled.

Before serving, heat the soup to simmering, add the chicken, remaining corn kernels and fresh herbs and cook until the meat is warmed through, about 3 to 5 minutes. Adjust the flavor with salt to taste and serve.

Glazed Baked Ham

SERVES 12 TO 14

THE BOUNDARY BETWEEN NORTH AND South blurs in this part of the country on several subjects, and one of them is ham. The southern tradition of country hams, smoked slowly in rural smokehouses or on family farms, sets a standard by which all other hams are judged. The capital of high-quality, commercial country ham production is Smithfield, Virginia, and the hams produced by the Smithfield company have tradition and heritage in every slice. But even if you don't have a genuine country ham, this recipe with its sweet, spicy glaze will transform any ham.

1 8- to 10-pound butt portion smoked cooked ham

12 whole cloves

1 cup dark brown sugar

¼ cup Dijon-style mustard

¼ cup maple syrup

Preheat the oven to 450°F. Place the ham on a metal rack in a roasting pan. Bake for 15 minutes. Remove the ham from the oven and lower the heat to 350°F. Insert the cloves into the skin at random intervals and return the ham to the oven.

In a small bowl, combine the brown sugar, mustard and maple syrup. When the ham has cooked for 1½ hours, take it out and coat it with the mixture. Return it to the oven and bake for ½ to 1 hour hour, until the internal temperature reaches 130°F.

Transfer the ham to a carving board, cut thin slices and serve.

Roast Duck with Red Cabbage

SERVES 4 TO 6

BLESSED WITH AN ABUNDANCE OF WILDLIFE, the mid-coastal region offered colonists a variety of foods in the streams, bays, ocean and forests around them. Hunting for ducks migrating in autumn along the great eastern flyways is a revered tradition that dates back to these early days. But commercially raised ducks are just as delicious in this recipe that honors the culinary traditions of the area's German immigrants. Cabbage and apples are a traditional combination used to make sauerkraut.

2 4-to-5 pound ducks

2 teaspoons salt

2 teaspoons freshly ground pepper

2 tablespoons dried sage

1 6-ounce can frozen apple juice concentrate, thawed

1 small red onion, thinly sliced

3 garlic cloves, minced

3 firm apples, peeled, cored, cut into eighths

1 teaspoon ground cloves

½ cup cider vinegar

4 cups shredded red cabbage

Preheat the oven to 475°F. Rinse and dry the ducks. Using a fork, poke holes all over them, being sure to pierce well into the layer of fat. Sprinkle the salt, pepper and sage in the ducks' cavities. Place in a deep roasting pan fitted with a metal rack.

Cook the ducks for 20 minutes, then remove from the oven to baste with some of the apple juice concentrate. Lower the heat to 350°F and return the ducks to the oven. Continue to roast for 1 hour.

While the ducks are roasting, prepare the cabbage and apples. Remove ⅓ cup of the duck fat that has melted onto the bottom of the roasting pan and pour into a large, deep pot. Add the onion and garlic and sauté over medium heat for 3 minutes. Add the apples and cloves and cook for another 5 minutes. Remove the apples and set them aside. Dissolve 2 ounces of the apple juice concentrate in 6 ounces of water and pour into the pot. Add the vinegar and red cabbage and bring to a boil over high heat. Lower the heat until the cabbage simmers, cover and cook for 45 minutes. Remove the lid, stir in the apples and continue to simmer until most of the liquid has evaporated.

When the leg joints of the ducks are loose, and the juices run slightly rosy, remove from the oven and let them rest for 15 minutes before carving. Place a bed of cabbage in the center of each plate. Carve the ducks into serving portions and place on top of the cabbage.

Free-Range Turkey with Port Sauce

SERVES 6

WILD TURKEYS, NATIVE TO eastern woodlands, were a food source first enjoyed by Native Americans in the region. Active and delicious, they bear little resemblance in appearance or taste to today's farm-raised turkeys. If possible, for the best flavor, choose a free-range turkey now available in a variety of sizes. Because free-range turkeys are not intentionally fattened-up, it is important to bard and baste the bird several times during roasting to keep the meat from drying out. "Bard" means tying a piece of bacon, pork fat, or beef suet that has been pounded flat to the turkey so it can add its natural fat and enrich the turkey's flavor. Remove and discard the barding fat before carving.

1 fresh free-range or wild 10- to 12-pound turkey

2 cups chicken broth

1 tablespoon freshly ground pepper

1 orange, halved

1 onion, quartered

1 tablespoon dried sage

4 strips bacon

¼ cup minced mushrooms

1 tablespoon minced shallots

¼ pound prosciutto, thinly sliced, diced

2 teaspoons cornstarch

½ cup medium-dry Port

Preheat the oven to 500°F. Rinse and pat dry the turkey. Snip off the tips of the wings and place them in a medium-size pot with the neck and the chicken broth. Set aside.

Sprinkle the pepper in the cavity of the bird. Place on a metal rack in a deep roasting pan. Squeeze the orange halves over the turkey and then place into the cavity along with the onion and sage. Drape the bacon across the breasts and secure with cotton string. Put in the oven and immediately reduce the heat to 375°F. Cover with a tent of aluminum foil and roast for 15 minutes per pound. Baste with the juices every 20 minutes.

While the turkey is roasting, bring the wings and neck in the chicken broth to a simmer over medium-low heat and cook for 2 hours. Add more broth or water as necessary to keep 2 cups of liquid.

When the turkey leg is loose and the juices coming from the turkey are clear, take the bird out of the oven and let it rest for 15 minutes.

Remove the bird to a carving board, cover with foil and place in a warm spot. Remove as much liquid fat from the roasting pan as possible. Place the pan on the stove over high heat. Add the mushrooms and shallots and cook for 2 minutes. Strain the chicken broth into the pan and bring to a boil. Boil, whisking vigorously to loosen any cooked-on bits from the pan. Strain through a fine sieve into a medium-size pot. Add the prosciutto and simmer for 5 minutes. Dissolve the cornstarch in the Port and slowly whisk into the strained sauce. Slowly bring the sauce to a boil over low heat, whisking constantly until it has thickened.

Remove the string and bacon from the turkey. Carve and serve alongside the Port sauce.

Potatoes and Sugar Snap Peas

SERVES 6 TO 8

THE FERTILE LOWLANDS OF THE MID-ATLANTIC states yield an amazing variety of garden produce. Whether from a small backyard garden or a sizable commercial operation, vegetables grown in this part of the country are among the best anywhere. This simple dish finds its roots in Pennsylvania Dutch culinary traditions where gardens were carefully tended to feed large families. It's bliss in early summer when the first tender sugar snap peas are ready to pick or just in at the farmer's market. Add new potatoes tossed in lots of butter and, like some folks, you may make this dish an entire meal.

½ pound small red new potatoes, scrubbed, thinly sliced

1 teaspoon salt

1 pound sugar snap peas (also known as Mennonite pod peas), strings removed

4 tablespoons unsalted butter

Place the potatoes in a large pot of cold, salted water and bring to a boil over high heat. Lower the heat to a gentle simmer and cook for 10 minutes. Add the sugar snap peas, return to a simmer and cook for 5 minutes. Drain and toss the potatoes and peas with the butter in a large bowl and serve.

Shoofly Pie

SERVES 6 TO 8

SWEET DESSERTS WERE ENJOYED IN America long before white sugar was readily available. This rich pie, believed to be Pennsylvania Dutch in origin, has a unique and fanciful name that first appeared in print in 1926. Some think the name may derive from the translation of a German word, but more likely it refers to the fact that the pie's exposed sweet surface had to be constantly fanned to keep flies away. Either way, its soft molasses filling and crumb topping is delectable. A dollop of whipped cream can add a luscious indulgence.

⅓ cup hot coffee

⅓ cup boiling water

½ teaspoon baking soda

½ cup blackstrap molasses

1 cup sifted flour

½ cup old-fashioned oatmeal

¼ teaspoon salt

¼ teaspoon ground cloves

¾ cup dark brown sugar

⅓ cup unsalted butter, cut into bits

1 9-inch prepared pie shell

Preheat the oven to 350°F. In a small bowl, combine the coffee, water, baking soda and molasses.

Using a food processor or blender, combine the flour, oatmeal, salt, cloves and brown sugar. Slowly add the butter and process until it resembles coarse meal.

Spread half of the crumb mix over the bottom of the pie shell. Pour the molasses mixture over it and top with the remaining crumb mix. Bake in the oven for 35 to 40 minutes. Cool on a metal rack and serve warm.

Gingerbread

SERVES 6 TO 8

MEDIEVAL MONKS PROBABLY WERE first to bake with ginger, using it in a heavy dark bread made from rye or wheat flour, honey and various spices. By the 1400s, this type of gingerbread was a staple throughout northern Europe. In the 1600s, eggs and butter or lard were added. This moist, spicy cake then traveled to America with the English colonists. Over the centuries, gingerbread has taken different forms. Sometimes it's studded with raisins and nuts, sometimes not. It can be cookies, cake or even biscuits, shaped, rolled or baked in a pan. But there's always a blending of fragrant spices and dark molasses, as in this scrumptious, old-fashioned cake version.

2	cups flour
½	cup whole wheat flour
1½	teaspoons baking soda
½	teaspoon salt
1¼	teaspoons ground ginger
1	teaspoon ground cinnamon
½	teaspoon ground cloves
½	teaspoon allspice
8	tablespoons unsalted butter, softened
½	cup sugar
1	egg
1	cup blackstrap molasses
1	cup boiling water
1	cup confectioner's sugar
1	tablespoon fresh lemon juice
1	tablespoon freshly grated gingerroot

Preheat the oven to 350°F. Coat a 9 x 9 x 2-inch baking pan with butter and line with waxed paper.

Over a medium bowl, sift together the first 8 ingredients. Using an electric mixer on high speed, beat the butter and sugar in a large bowl until fluffy, about 5 minutes. Beat in the egg. Combine the molasses and boiling water and add it to the butter mixture, alternating with the dry ingredients, until they are all combined. Pour the batter into the prepared pan and bake for 50 minutes. Remove to a metal rack and cool slightly before turning out of the pan.

In a small mixing bowl, whisk together the confectioner's sugar, lemon juice and grated ginger until smooth. Spread over the cooled cake. Cut into squares or rectangles and serve.

Mid-Atlantic

Index